The Journey of Reconciliation

The Journey of Reconciliation

Groaning for New Creation in Africa

Emmanuel Katongole

ORBIS BOOKS
Maryknoll, New York 10545

ORBIS BOOKS
Maryknoll, New York 10545

Fathers and Brothers
MARYKNOLL™

Founded in 1970, Orbis Books endeavors to publish works that enlighten the mind, nourish the spirit, and challenge the conscience. The publishing arm of the Maryknoll Fathers and Brothers, Orbis seeks to explore the global dimensions of the Christian faith and mission, to invite dialogue with diverse cultures and religious traditions, and to serve the cause of reconciliation and peace. The books published reflect the views of their authors and do not represent the official position of the Maryknoll Society. To learn more about Maryknoll and Orbis Books, please visit our website at www.maryknollsociety.org.

Manufactured in the United States of America

Library of Congress Cataloging-in-Publication Data

Names: Katongole, Emmanuel, 1960- author.
Title: The journey of reconciliation : groaning for a new creation in Africa / Emmanuel Katongole.
Description: Maryknoll : Orbis Books, 2017. | Includes bibliographical references and index.
Identifiers: LCCN 2017027260 (print) | LCCN 2017027562 (ebook) | ISBN 9781608337156 (e-book) | ISBN 9781626982505 (pbk.)
Subjects: LCSH: Reconciliation—Religious aspects—Christianity. | Christianity—Africa.
Classification: LCC BT738.27 (ebook) | LCC BT738.27 .K378 2017 (print) | DDC 261.8096—dc23
LC record available at https://lccn.loc.gov/2017027260

To all the leaders of the Africa Great Lakes Initiative who have taught me most of what I know and have come to believe about the journey of reconciliation.

Contents

**Part III: Improvising New Creation:
On Being Ambassadors of Reconciliation in a Divided World**

On Discovering Reconciliation

A growing interest in reconciliation can be observed from the number of books that have been published on the topic just in the recent past.[1] The range of titles confirms that the interest in reconciliation is shared not only by scholars in theology and religious studies, but by politicians, psychologists, peace activists, and scholars in the humanities as well as the social sciences. What the wide-ranging interest in reconciliation confirms, moreover, is the longing for peace and healing in our increasingly violent and conflict-ridden world. In the face of much personal and social brokenness, we are eager to try out any skills, techniques, and strategies that promise an end to hostility. Reconciliation is often depicted as one such mechanism or process that promises not only the healing of past hostilities but also a path to a future beyond

---

[1]For a sample, see John Paul Lederach, *Reconcile: Conflict Transformation for Ordinary Christians* (Harrisburg, VA: Herald Press, 2014); Brenda Salter McNeil, *Roadmap to Reconciliation: Moving Communities into Unity, Wholeness and Justice* (Downers Grove, IL: InterVarsity Press, 2016). Pope Benedict, *Africae Munus: Post-synodal Exhortation on the Church in Africa in Service to Reconciliation, Justice, and Peace* (2012). A. E. Orobator, ed., *Reconciliation, Justice, and Peace: The Second African Synod* (Maryknoll, NY: Orbis Books, 2011); Leo W. Riegert, Jill Scott, and Jack Shuler, eds., *Thinking and Practicing Reconciliation: Teaching and Learning through Literary Responses to Conflict* (Newcastle upon Tyne, UK: Cambridge Scholars Publishing, 2014); Erin Daly and Jeremy Sarkin, *Reconciliation in Divided Societies: Finding Common Ground*, Pennsylvania Studies in Human Rights (Philadelphia: University of Pennsylvania Press, 2010); Benazir Bhutto, *Reconciliation: Islam, Democracy, and the West* (New York: Harper Collins, 2008), as well my and Chris Rice's *Reconciling All Things: A Christian Vision of Justice, Peace and Healing* (Downers Grove, IL: InterVarsity Press, 2008).

the cycles of revenge and hatred. There is a lot that is positive about the various recommendations of reconciliation as a strategy for personal, social, and political healing. However, what is often not clear from the various recommendations and programs of reconciliation is the role that Christian faith actually plays in these reconciliation efforts. For even when it is acknowledged that the notion of reconciliation has a long history within the Christian tradition, reconciliation programs, and recommendations, it seems often to have very little to do with one's Christian convictions and faith journey. As a result, it is often not clear what difference, if any, Christian faith makes in the understanding and pursuit of reconciliation.

This book sets out to make explicit the difference that Christian faith makes in the way one understands and engages reconciliation, and what that looks like on the continent of Africa. The central conviction of the book is that from a Christian point of view, reconciliation is a journey—not in the first place a journey that one undertakes, but God's journey with creation. This journey, which begins with the creation of the world (Genesis), is propelled forward by God's promise—nay, commitment—to restore fallen creation and humanity to its original designs. It is this journey that scripture bears witness to, and thus the prophets of the Old Testament constantly call the people back into the reality of God's shalom, even as they announce God's promise of a "new" covenant and a "new" creation. The good news that Christians celebrate is that in the Christ event, this promise has been realized, thus bringing God's journey with creation to a decisive moment.

No one has expressed this conviction as clearly as Paul in the second letter to the Corinthians, when he talks about God's ongoing act of reconciliation as the process through which God has made possible the gift of a new creation. "For anyone in Christ," Paul writes, "there's a new creation. . . . The old is gone, the new is here. All this is from God, who through Christ reconciled us to himself . . . that is, in Christ God was reconciling the world to himself, not counting their trespasses against them" (2 Cor 5:17–19). Involved in this declaration by Paul is the conviction that reconciliation is at the heart of God's journey with creation (God was reconciling the world) as the ongoing process through which God renews creation and makes possible the reality of the new creation. But while Paul talks about "new creation" as a gift ("all this is from God") which is experienced by "anyone in Christ," he also talks about God "entrusting us" with the message of reconciliation, and (in v. 20) exhorts Christians to live as "ambassadors" of God's reconciliation. What this means is that for Christians, God's ongoing journey of reconciliation is at once a gift and an invitation. Christians find themselves at once recipients of the gift of God's reconciling activity in the world and at the same time the subject of an invitation to be ambassadors of that gift. This is in brief the theory—the metaphysics, if you like—of reconciliation. This is the story of reconciliation and how the Christian fits within this story of God's reconciling journey. The challenge facing us here, as with any theological work, is not so much the articulation of theory but the display of the social, practical, and ecclesiological implications of this theory of reconciliation in its historical concreteness. The challenge facing us is one of giving an account of what it means for the Christian to find himself or herself at the intersection of the gift and the invitation of the new creation, or put differently, an account of how Christian life is shaped in between the already and not yet of God's new creation. Specifically for this book, the challenge is to show what the gift and the invitation of reconciliation concretely look like on the continent of Africa where the realities of civil war, ethnic violence, and poverty seem to be endemic.

This is what I intend to do in this collection of essays, *The Journey of Reconciliation: Groaning for New Creation in Africa*, in which I display the social, practical, and ecclesiological dimensions of the journey of reconciliation in Africa. Even though portions were originally conceived at different times and for various audiences, all the essays in *The Journey of Reconciliation* reflect the basic conviction of reconciliation as both a gift and an invitation.

From 2005 to 2011, I served as founding co-director of the Duke Center for Reconciliation. Since most of what I have learned about the journey of reconciliation was shaped within this context as well as in the context of my work with Christian leaders in East Africa, there might be no better way to talk about the journey of reconciliation in Africa than to tell the story of how

I came to discover reconciliation as a rich theological category, indeed the very heart of the Gospel. The discovery proved to be revolutionary in that it would totally reshape my vision of theology as well as my work as a theologian. But since the story of the founding of the Duke Center for Reconciliation has been told in *Reconciling All Things: A Christian Vision of Justice, Peace, and Healing* there seems to be no need to repeat it. What I wish to do here, however, is to point to three crucial gifts that came with the invitation to become a founding co-director of the Duke Center for Reconciliation as a way to highlight the shared content, context, and methodology of the essays in this volume.

On Discovering the Gift of Reconciliation: A Personal Story

In October 2004, Chris Rice and I had just returned from the 2004 Lausanne Forum for World Evangelization in Pattaya, Thailand, as part of an issue group on reconciliation. Working with Chris and more than fifty leaders from around the world before and at the Lausanne Forum in Pattaya had been a unique opportunity. It had not only brought me in contact with some of the most amazing Christian leaders in the Evangelical world, many of whom have remained close friends; it had extended my appreciation of "reconciliation" beyond my native Catholic understanding, which tended to associate reconciliation almost exclusively with the sacrament of reconciliation. Even then I did not think that reconciliation would become a major focus in my work. As far as I was concerned, Lausanne was a significant forum, but an event nonetheless. I was ready to carry on with my research on politics and violence in Africa. I was therefore greatly surprised when Greg Jones, the then dean of the Duke Divinity School, asked me if I would be interested to continue to work with Chris and establish a center for reconciliation at Duke Divinity School. While I was honored by the invitation and the opportunity to work with Chris, whom I had come to know more over the course of the year, seemed exciting, I turned down the invitation. Basically, there were two reasons why I did not want to lead a reconciliation initiative at Duke. Ironically, each of these hesitations would come to yield a unique set of gifts, which are reflected in the content and context of the essays in this volume.

Content: The Journey of Reconciliation

The first reason why I had initially turned down Greg's invitation to become founding co-director of a center for reconciliation was that even though in *Reconciliation as God's Mission*, the small statement (document) which our issue group had prepared for Lausanne, we sought to locate the evangelical emphasis on "ministry of reconciliation" within a primary understanding of reconciliation as God's gift and mission in the world, this was a minority position. The predominant interest in reconciliation ministries was driven by an activist impulse of assumed reconciliation experts or "reconcilers" who traveled to different trouble spots of conflict and division around the world offering advice and skills of how to reconcile. I did not think I had either the skills or the temperament of a "reconciler." And I told Greg so. While Greg listened patiently to my concerns, he also encouraged me to take the time to reflect more on Paul's words in his Second Letter to the Corinthians (2 Cor 5:17–20), and to imagine a center that would flow out of that text.

Following Greg's recommendation, Chris and I undertook a five-day retreat at Trinity Center, an Episcopal Retreat Center on Emerald Isle, in North Carolina. On the retreat, as Chris and I prayed and studied the text of 2 Corinthians 5:17–20, and shared convictions as we walked the North Carolina beach, a number of convictions became clear about reconciliation, which a center for reconciliation could help illuminate. Most of these convictions were connected to the overriding vision of reconciliation as a journey—God's journey with creation, into which the Christian is invited. In a context where everyone was calling for more skills, techniques, and programs that promised to solve the world's brokenness, an opportunity to recover a theological vision of reconciliation located within the context of God's story became exciting. For one thing that becomes obvious at the retreat is that abstracted from God's story, the notion of reconciliation not only remains vague, it loses its character as a unique gift to the world. But the more reconciliation is connected to God's story and work in the world, we felt, the more urgent the invitation to be "ambassadors" of reconciliation in a broken world becomes. By the end of the retreat, it was not only clear that I would take on the responsibility of co-founding a center for reconciliation, I was also deeply excited by the unique opportunity and possibilities of this leadership role. If before I had turned down the invitation because of my distaste for the activist impulse of reconciliation ministries, which did not seem to have any theological moorings, now I was excited about the opportunity to reshape the Christian understanding of reconciliation by grounding it within an adequate theological context and narrative. And so, over the next few years as Chris and I set up the center and designed its various programs, we were guided by the basic theological conviction of reconciliation as a journey grounded in God's story. As we sought to make explicit and seed this conviction in the various programs of the center's work, five key themes emerged as an outline of the gifts and disciplines that shape the Christian journey of reconciliation in the world.

First, *new creation* as the telos or the "toward what" of the journey of reconciliation. In talking about reconciliation the end must always be kept in focus; otherwise reconciliation comes to name any endless number of attempts to address the world's brokenness, whose ultimate goal however remains unclear. Scripture and other Christian practices such as worship shape the imagination and memory of the Christian to keep focused on the big picture and the end to which the journey of reconciliation leads.

Second, the journey of reconciliation is grounded in *lament*. For even as one keeps in mind the gift of new creation, one is constantly confronted by the realities of what's going on here and now—realities of violence, conflict, poverty, divisions, and so on. The discipline and strange gift of lament allows one to stand on this ground of pain without giving in to despair. Moreover, the discipline of lament compels one to investigate the deep social, political, and economic structures that shape histories of violence, injustice, poverty, and divisions around the world. Without such sustained critical analysis, talk of reconciliation becomes simply a panacea, a way of healing the wound of "my people lightly, saying, Peace, peace; when there is no peace" (Jer 6:14).

Third, reconciliation is about *hope* in the world. The gift of new creation means that even in places of deep brokenness God's reconciling work is ongoing. Even in the midst of the world's pain,

God continues to plant seeds of hope and to give birth to the new creation. As Isaiah says, "See, I am doing a new thing! Now it springs up; do you not perceive it? I am making a way in the wilderness and streams in the wasteland" (Is 43:19). Accordingly, a key part of the theological task in relation to reconciliation has to do with our ability to "see" hope, and thus, be able as the First Letter of Saint Peter exhorts, "to give account of the hope" (1 Pt 3:15) that is around us. The way Chris and I understood this charge was that a great part of the work of the Center for Reconciliation would be to tell stories of hope. Of course, it was also clear to us that the kind of stories that would shape the work of the center would be those that illumined not only God's story in the world but also the church as God's new language of hope in a broken world. This ecclesiological dimension of reconciliation was very clear to us from the very start and meant that our work would have to highlight the role and mission of the church—why the church matters for reconciliation. But it also meant that an adequate ecclesiological account would have to point not to an idealized church, but the church in its complex history, pointing to both the church's limits and possibilities, its complicity in violence as well as its possibility to radiate a "different world" in the midst of violence and division.

Fourth, reconciliation requires *leadership*. The invitation to be ambassadors of God's new creation in the world points to the "work" of reconciliation in the world as the Christian finds himself or herself in that "sluggish between" of the already and not yet of God's new creation. This observation pointed to the significance of forming leaders with various capacities for scriptural imagination, mediation, negotiation, patience, and all forms of skillful advocacy and improvisation necessary for the invitation to live as an ambassador of a new creation.

Fifth, reconciliation involves a personal journey of *conversion*. Even as reconciliation involves endless advocacy for peace, justice, and the end of war in the world, it is deeply a personal journey. Reconciliation involves not only intimacy with God but requires the cultivation of spiritual and other resources necessary to sustain the journey over the long haul.

In the end, these five gifts and disciplines became the content that shaped my and Chris's work at the Center for Reconciliation as we sought "to inspire, form, and support leaders, communities, and congregations to live as ambassadors of reconciliation" (CFR mission). This is the same content that is worked through the various essays in this collection. *The Journey of Reconciliation* is about the imagination (new creation), lament, hope, leadership, and spirituality that sustain the journey of reconciliation in Africa.

The Context: The Great Lakes Initiative

The other reason why I had initially turned down Greg's invitation to spearhead a center for reconciliation had to do with my concern that the center would be dominated by questions of racial reconciliation. Having been at Duke for three years, I had come to realize the extent to which "race" was the primary lens through which not simply black-white relationships, but Christianity as a whole was viewed in the United States, particularly in the South. It was therefore obvious to me that for an African like myself to work with Chris, a white Evangelical Christian, who had spent seventeen years in Mississippi living in an intentional interracial community and who was a national leader in racial reconciliation, our partnership and work would immediately be perceived as simply an initiative for "racial reconciliation." Important as the issue of racial reconciliation no doubt is, I thought the center's scope ought to be broader. Moreover, given my background, I was not sure that I was the right person to take on the challenges of racial reconciliation in America. Beyond this, I was concerned that a center of reconciliation in North Carolina (the South) would not only be dominated by issues of racial reconciliation but that its focus would be the American context. I worried that assuming leadership of such a center would simply distract me from what I understood to be the focus of my work and research, namely the continent of Africa.

In response to this concern Greg assured me that it would be up to me and Chris to determine the center's programs according to our geographic interests and expertise. At any rate, he hoped that the center would be able to support and advance my work and scholarship on Africa. This is how from the start, the African

Great Lakes Initiative (GLI) became a core program of the center. Every year the GLI organizes a leadership institute, a five-day program that outlines a theological vision of reconciliation, offers participants an opportunity to interact with and learn from some of the most remarkable and dynamic Christian leaders in East Africa, while equipping participants with specific theological and practical skills for their work. To be sure, the growth of the GLI to this dynamic program of learning, interaction, and transformation in Eastern Africa has itself been a miraculous journey. For when Chris and I first convened thirty Christian leaders from five countries in Eastern Africa near Kampala in November 2006, all we wanted to do was to cast a theological vision of reconciliation and to invite leaders, coming from some of the most painful and violence-ridden contexts, including Rwanda, Eastern Congo, Burundi, and Northern Uganda, to share their stories of both lament and of hope living and working in those geographies. At the end of this three-day gathering, the leaders invited us to convene a similar meeting every year, and thus create a space where Christian leaders in the region could connect both with the theological vision that drives their work and with one another, and be equipped with skills to sustain their work.[2] And so, working with local partner organizations, we found ourselves convening a gathering of the East African leaders every year, deepening the theological content and expanding the number of leaders. To date, the GLI is one of the most dynamic, ecumenically diverse, theologically based, practically oriented, and regionally rooted organizations that brings together over 120 leaders in its annual five-day leadership institute.

Looking back, having an opportunity to work with our East African partners and leaders to shape the vision of the GLI and to design its content and programs is one of the most precious gifts of my work with the Duke Center for Reconciliation. No doubt, it involved a lot of work, numerous frustrations, and a number of trips back and forth between Duke and East Africa. However,

---

[2]The stated mission of the Great Lakes Initiative (GLI) is to "mobilize restless Christian leaders from across the Great Lakes region of Africa, create a space for their transformation, and empower them to participate in God's mission of reconciliation in their own communities, organizations, and nations" (https:// divinity.duke.edu).

it not only helped confirm the vision of reconciliation as at once a gift and an invitation, but it also offered numerous glimpses of how the intersection of gift and invitation, the sluggish between of the already and not yet of reconciliation, concretely looks like within the East African landscape. If I had initially turned down the invitation to lead a reconciliation initiative because I worried that that initiative would distract from my work and research on Africa, the opposite happened. My work with the center not only deepened my research and engagement in Africa, it shaped it in dynamic and exciting ways through the community of the leaders of the African Great Lakes Initiative. This is partly the reason why even after I left the leadership of the Center for Reconciliation and Duke University in 2012, and moved on to the Kroc Institute at the University of Notre Dame, I continue to be part of the GLI, and a regular presence at the annual leadership institute. Without a community like the GLI and the stories of both pain and hope shared and represented by the different leaders and communities of the GLI, I would not know what the claim that "God has reconciled the world" concretely means.

Accordingly, if the convictions and stories in these essays emerged in the context of my work with the Center for Reconciliation, they were specifically tested out and confirmed through my interaction and work with African leaders through the GLI. Every time I receive an invitation to speak or write on reconciliation, whether for an academic, congregational, or ministerial audience, as I work out the theoretical framework or a particular dimension of reconciliation, I find myself drawing from the experience and stories from the Great Lakes Region to fill in the content of what the journey of reconciliation concretely looks like.

The Gift of Stories

If the content and context of the essays in the *Journey of Reconciliation* reflect unique gifts associated with my discovery of a substantive and theologically thick notion of reconciliation and of a community, they reflect another significant gift—of stories. Prior to 2005, my work remained largely theoretical. Coming out of a philosophical background of a PhD in philosophy from Leuven, I investigated the conditions of possibility and the social histories that made violence, tribalism, and poverty enduring realities within the social imagination of Africa.[3] Even as I pointed to the need for "interruption" and "alternatives" to this imagination, and the role that Christianity can play in this effort, I neither had a clear sense of the big picture or the telos of this Christian interruption nor offered any examples of what that concretely looked like. What the notion of reconciliation was able to offer was the social imaginary or the "toward what" of the interruption or alternative I was calling for. At the same time, my work with the leaders in the East Africa Great Lakes region made available the stories, both of pain and hope, which confirmed the journey and possibility of reconciliation in its contextual and concrete dimensions. This is how reconciliation saved my scholarship—by offering it a much needed theological, contextual, and practical dimension. As a result, with the notion of reconciliation, my work became decisively narrative,[4] a fact that is reflected in *The Journey of Reconciliation*, which is shaped around stories.

It is important, however to understand that I do not use stories in a facile or anecdotal sense. Stories are at the very heart of the theological project. And so the use of stories and the way the stories function in *The Journey of Reconciliation* reflects substantive methodological, epistemological, and practical convictions, which came to be shaped and honed in the context of my work at the Duke Center for Reconciliation and with the leaders in the East African region. To get a full sense of why and how stories matter for my scholarship, it is helpful to outline the methodological, epistemological, and practical dimensions of stories in the essays in *The Journey of Reconciliation*.

First, in terms of methodology, from early on in our work with the center, as we engaged various constituencies—students, faculty, and practitioners in congregations and ministries of reconcili-

---

[3]See my *Beyond Universal Reason: The Relation between Religion and Ethics in the Work of Stanley Hauerwas* (Notre Dame, IN: University of Notre Dame Press, 2000), and *A Future for Africa: Critical Essays in Christian Social Imagination* (Scranton, PA: University of Scranton Press, 2005).

[4]See, e.g., my *Mirror to the Church: Resurrecting Faith after Genocide in Rwanda* (Grand Rapids, MI: Zondervan, 2009), *The Sacrifice of Africa: A Political Theology for Africa* (Grand Rapids, MI: Eerdmans, 2011), and *Stories from Bethany: On the Faces of the Church in Africa* (Nairobi: Paulines, 2012)

ation around the world—Chris and I discovered that an adequate conversation about reconciliation must bring together at least three forms of knowledge: theological, contextual, and practical. We came to refer to this as the *Word Made Flesh* methodology. *Word*: "In the beginning was the Word . . ." is a reminder that a conversation about reconciliation must begin with and is shaped around the story of God, which Christians encounter in scripture and through the Christian tradition. *Made Flesh:* Through the Incarnation the Word became flesh at a particular time (history) and place (Nazareth), a reminder that history and context matter. Among other things, a conversation of reconciliation involves a critical reading of the histories that shape the particular contexts and places within which the journey of reconciliation is engaged. *Dwelt Among Us:* a reflection on reconciliation must engage the practical skills, stories, and patterns that confirm that the Word has become flesh not simply in our minds, but has come to "dwell among us"—thus affecting the way we see the world and live in it. Accordingly, a conversation on reconciliation must point to stories, examples, and practical models of lives and communities that confirm that indeed the Word was made flesh and has come to dwell among us.

The three do not constitute three separate forms of inquiry, but three moments of one inquiry or conversation about reconciliation which is at once theological, contextual, and practical. Each of these moments revolves around "story": with the story of God and stories of scripture driving the theological moment, the (hi)stories of the politics and economics of places driving the contextual moment, and the stories of individuals and communities driving the practical moment of reflection. What I try to do in each of the essays in *The Journey of Reconciliation* is to bring the three sets of stories into conversation and to display the theological, social, and practical implications of this conversation in relation to the gift and invitation of reconciliation in Africa.

Second, the use of stories in *The Journey of Reconciliation* involves an epistemological claim—namely, that the nature and structure of reality is revealed through stories. Thus the very point of the gift of New Creation within which the story of reconciliation operates is to invite Christians into a distinct epistemology, which is to say a distinct way of seeing or knowing reality. But since the truth of this distinct way cannot be known apart from the lives of the individuals and communities it shapes, stories provide both the argument and evidence. In this connection, the stories of individuals and communities captured in the essays in *The Journey of Reconciliation* provide the most persuasive argument and evidence that what Paul claims—namely, that "new creation is here"—can be said to be true in Africa. The realization of this insight had far-reaching implications for my scholarship. If, as I said, before 2004 my scholarship was largely theoretical, in the context of my work on reconciliation, it not only took on a hitherto missing practical dimension, its orientation shifted. If before I looked for stories to confirm theoretical assumptions, now I began to see that my task as a scholar was to display the theoretical, theological, and ecclesiological dimensions of the stories, which were the decisive evidence of the kind of lives shaped by and through the journey of reconciliation. In this case stories became the "glue" that tie both the theoretical and practical dimensions of my work, such that I do not have to feel the need to prioritize one over the other. Accordingly, the essays in this collection display the kind of systematic-practical theology that has become the hallmark of my scholarship.

Finally, with this epistemological commitment to narrative also came a broadening of the audience for my scholarship. Before 2015, I wrote for and spoke to primarily an academic audience. But as co-director of the Center for Reconciliation even as I continued to teach graduate classes at Duke and participated in the usual academic conferences, I was also invited to speak at various audiences of Christian practitioners at churches, ministry conferences, colleges, and gatherings and institutes hosted by the CFR. I found myself moving back and forth between two worlds: the world of academic scholarship, on the one hand, and the world of practitioners, on the other. I began to see my task as a theologian as one of bridging these two worlds, which are often kept apart and at times even seek to exclude each other. This required me to learn to speak and write in a simple and straightforward manner and style accessible to both audiences. But as an African Catholic priest working at a Methodist divinity school in America, co-leading a center with a Protestant Reformed Christian, and working closely with mainline, evangelical, and nondenominational Christians, my writing and scholarship also needed to bridge these audiences. I found that using stories, in their theological, contextual, and practical dimensions offered a most effective way to do so in a way that draws both scholars and practitioners, Catholics and Protestants, mainline and evangelicals into a sustained conversation about the journey of reconciliation. My hope is that these various audiences, in Africa as well as in the West and beyond will find the essays in *The Journey of Reconciliation* to be both engaging and provocative of further conversation.

Book Outline and Argument

The Journey of Reconciliation brings together eleven essays that portray different dimensions of what it means for Christians in Africa to receive the gift and invitation of reconciliation in the midst of the stubborn realities of war, poverty, and violence that characterize their daily living. A few of the essays have previously been published, and I am grateful to the publishers for the permission to include them in this collection. Many of the essays originated as invited public lectures. Although I have edited them to fit within the scope and central argument of the book, I have tried as much as possible to retain their original flavor and context as public lectures. My hope is that retaining the format and tone of each essay's original context offers the reader an extra opportunity to appreciate the historical, occasional, and piecemeal nature of the journey of reconciliation itself.

The book is divided into three parts. Part I, "Reconciling All Things," which is the more theoretical section of the book, outlines a theological vision of reconciliation as God's journey with creation which involves both gift and mission. Chapter 1, "Reconciliation: The Gift of, and the Invitation into, Another World," is an extended reflection on the text of 2 Corinthians 5:17–20 and outlines the exegetical, theological, and practical implications of the text. The chapter makes clear that what Paul is talking about in this text is the reality of another world—the new creation—that God has made possible in our midst through the process of reconciliation. Christian worship in general and the sacramental life of the church in particular allow the Christian to step into that drama, relive it, and keep one's eyes on the gift and the invitation as well as the telos of its journey.

The theme of stepping into the drama of God's reconciling journey is picked up in Chapter 2, "Reconciling Justice." Using the interest in transitional justice mechanisms as a lens, I highlight the limitations of the search for political justice in Africa. The limitations point to the violence that is wired, so to say, within the social imagery of nation-state politics in Africa. These foundational visions have to be reinvented if any transition into a new political future in Africa is to be conceived. Angelina Atyam's story of forgiveness is an attempt to reinvent this social imaginary by offering a different ontology, the self-sacrificing and reconciling love of God, as the foundation of political life.

In Chapter 3, "The End of Words," against the background of the 1994 Rwanda genocide, I describe the "silence" of postgenocide Rwanda as the lament over the destruction of the foundations of human and social existence. That is why reconciliation, in the wake of the genocide, involves not simply bringing Hutu and Tutsi together, not only forgiving enemies, but re-creating the very foundations of humanity and social existence that were shattered through the genocide. This is what makes reconciliation more than a human enterprise, a gift, the work of God.

Chapter 4, "Reconciling *Africae Munus*," is an extended reflection on the post-synodal apostolic exhortation *Africae Munus*. In this chapter I argue that although Pope Benedict, in *Africae Munus,* following the second Synod of Bishops for Africa, urges the African church to pursue reconciliation and seek justice and peace, the vision of reconciliation remains implicit. The chapter makes explicit the vision of reconciliation behind *Africae Munus* and argues that once the vision of a God who "reconciles all things" is made explicit, the call of *Africae Munus* becomes even more urgent and pressing in Africa.

In Part II, "For the Life of the World: The Church as Sacrament of God's Reconciliation in the World," I explore the ecclesiological dimension of reconciliation and provide different portraits of why and how the church matters for reconciliation in Africa. In Chapter 5, "Parables of a 'New We': Thinking Theologically about Identity," I argue that if the gift and telos of reconciliation characterize the new creation, then God's mission is to form a new people in the world, bringing together even those who were once far apart into the one household of God. The chapter provides different parables of the church as God's new people ("new we") in the context of Africa's ethnic divisions.

In Chapter 6, "On Learning to Betray One's People," I extend the reflections on identity of the previous chapter through a missiological reflection on Ephesian communities and identities. I use the story of the seminarians at Buta in Burundi, who refused to separate themselves into groups of Hutu and Tutsi and were thus killed, to show that the church's call as God's new people redefines the very notion of who one's people are. The chapter displays the subversive, practical, social, and political character of the church in the context of Africa's politics of ethnic violence.

Chapter 7, "'Threatened with Resurrection': The Terrible Gift of Martyrs," argues that martyrs provide the most concrete, dynamic, and exemplary case of the journey of reconciliation. Accordingly, the African church offers no more important witness of the hope of God's reconciliation in the world than in its memory of the martyrs. The chapter explores this dangerous memory of the martyrs and how that memory constantly invites and threatens the church, the African church in particular, with the gift and mission of reconciliation.

Part III, "Improvising New Creation: On Being Ambassadors of Reconciliation in a Divided World," uses the stories of select faith peace activists to illumine the elements of personal journey, spirituality, and practical disciplines that sustain the life and work of an ambassador of reconciliation. Using Sam Wells's notion of improvisation as a framing device, I argue that what is going on in these different lives, more than any application of technical skills or mechanisms of reconciliation, is a form of improvisation grounded in the formed habits and patterns of living within the Christian story. But since even the personal journey of reconciliation is only made possible and is at the same time a reflection of the church as the primary recipient of the gift and mission of reconciliation, the stories in this chapter provide different portraits or radiances of the church's reconciling mission in the world.

In Chapter 8, "Archbishop John Baptist Odama and the Politics of Baptism in Northern Uganda," I tell the story of Archbishop John Baptist Odama of Gulu in Northern Uganda and his work for peace in the context of the LRA violence. Odama's exemplary leadership, I argue, cannot make sense outside the context of his call as a priest, a call that is renewed through the daily practices of prayer and his weekly retreat before the Blessed Sacrament.

The same can be said about Archbishop Emmanuel Kataliko in Congo, whose story I tell in Chapter 9, "Archbishop Emmanuel Kataliko and the 'Excess of Love' in Bukavu." The chapter forms part of a broader argument that in the context of Africa's political violence, there is no more pressing challenge for New Evangelization than the search for a different, nonviolent basis for social existence in Africa. This is what the story of Archbishop Kataliko's life and work in the Congo is about. Both in Butembo and particularly in Bukavu, through his pastoral leadership, Kataliko invited his audience into a new vision of society grounded in the story of God's nonviolent and reconciling love.

I describe Maggy Barankitse's life in Chapter 10, "A Blood Thicker Than Tribalism." Maggy Barankitse and Maison Shalom in Burundi reveal a similar example of innovative leadership that seeks to realize a new vision of society grounded in God's reconciling love. For Maggy, founding Maison Shalom at the height of Burundi's civil wars in the 1990s was an attempt to offer an alternative to Burundi's politics of ethnic violence. Thus, Maison Shalom was and remains an example of improvisation of the reconciling love of God that is encountered and renewed every day through the Eucharist.

The last chapter, "Field Hospital: The Compassion of Jo and Lyn Lusi in Eastern Congo," makes explicit the interconnections of ecclesiology, evangelism, and politics, and serves as a good conclusion to the book. Using Pope Francis's image of the church as a field hospital, the essay explores the church's ministry of reconciliation in the context of the violence and social disruption in Eastern Congo. In the very process of healing wounds, the essay argues, the church (as field hospital) initiates new social possibilities that reflect God's healing and reconciling presence in the world. The story of Dr. Jo and Lyn Lusi and their work with HEAL Africa and its holistic ministry in and around Goma exemplifies this mission in its personal, ecclesial, and political dimensions.

The overall objective of this section and indeed of the whole book is to confirm reconciliation as the gift and invitation into another world—the world of new creation. Responding to the invitation involves a personal journey. But the deeper that one gets drawn into the drama of this new creation, the more one is able to discover new possibilities of living in the world and of responding to its patterns of violence and division with alternatives that confirm not only the possibility but the presence of a different world. It is this world of God's reconciling love that the church as God's new people is invited into, so as to experience it and at the same time make it available in today's world. It is this world of God's reconciling journey that Paul points to, using the language of "new creation," and celebrates even as he exhorts the Christians in Corinth to live as its ambassadors: "anyone in Christ, new creation is here. The old is gone, the new is here. All this is from God who has reconciled the world to himself" (2 Cor 5:17). *The Journey of Reconciliation* provides a glimpse of this Good News in its many dimensions, including its possibilities and frustrations on the African continent.

PART I

RECONCILING ALL THINGS

1

Reconciliation

The Gift of, and the Invitation into, Another World

I am grateful to Professor Timothy O'Malley, the director for the Notre Dame Center for Liturgy, for inviting me to speak at this symposium on liturgy and healing. Tim's invitation to me was specific: "We are asking you to address a theology of reconciliation, one that might renew the imagination of our guests regarding what it means to participate fully, consciously, and actively in the rite of penance." As I thought about the charge to me, it became clear that the best way to help Christians, especially Catholic Christians, to "participate fully, consciously, and actively in the rite of penance" and overall in the sacramental life of the church is to sketch a vision of reconciliation that involves but goes beyond the sacrament of penance. I am well aware that Catholics tend to think about reconciliation almost exclusively as a personal and inner experience of getting right with God. There is, of course, a basic truth connected to this essentially spiritual dimension— namely, that we are a sinful people in need of God's forgiveness, which we receive in the sacrament of penance. However, to speak about reconciliation exclusively, or even primarily, in this manner does not do full justice to the rich gift and dynamic invitation that reconciliation is. In other words, although the notion of

---

This essay was originally given as a lecture at the Symposium on Liturgy and Healing Institute for Church life. University of Notre Dame, Indiana, June 16–19, 2013.

reconciliation involves spiritual healing and the forgiveness of sins, the range of its meaning is much broader and its vision is far more radical. As I understand it, reconciliation has to do with the reality of another world—the new creation—that God has made possible in our midst.[1] Within this broad context of new creation, the sacramental life of the church in general and the rite of penance in particular takes on a fresh and renewed significance.

My presentation has two parts. In the first part, using the text of 2 Corinthians 5:17–20, I sketch a vision of reconciliation as the gift of a new creation and the invitation to enter that new creation. In the second part, I draw specific conclusions and connections between the broad vision of reconciliation sketched out for Christian living in general and for the sacramental life of the church in particular.

Another World Is Here—New Creation

When I think of reconciliation in its most broad conception, a personal experience in the summer of 2010 comes to mind. My flight from JFK to Brussels had been delayed. I would miss my connection, and since there were only three flights to Entebbe each week, I would have to wait for two days in Brussels for my

---

[1] In the broad Christian context, one notices a resurgent interest in reconciliation as a specific ministry of "reconcilers"—of people committed to mend historical social divisions of racism, class, poverty, gender. In this connection, the life and work of Dr. John Perkins of Mississippi has inspired many ministries and initiatives of "reconciliation" within the broader evangelical world in the United States. See, for example, John M. Perkins, *A Quiet Revolution: The Christian Response to Human Need, a Strategy for Today,* rev. ed. (1976; Pasadena, CA: Urban Family Publications, 1990); Spenser Perkins and Chris Rice, *More Than Equals: Racial Healing for the Sake of the Gospel,* rev. ed. (1993; Downers Grove, IL: InterVarsity Press, 2000). Within the academic world, reconciliation has also increasingly grown popular in the field of peace studies, as a process or skill for mediation, an integral dimension of strategic peace building, or a process of restorative justice in the wake of mass atrocity and violence. For a more recent argument in this direction, see Dan Philpott, *Just and Unjust Peace: An Ethic of Political Reconciliation* (Oxford: Oxford University Press, 2015). Although there is much to appreciate about this interest in personal, social, and political reconciliation, to the extent that many of these initiatives assume and build onto the realism of the way things are, they fall short of the full imaginative, and even subversive, potential of the Pauline notion of reconciliation as the irruption of a new creation within the reality of the world as we know it.

connection. The service representative could, however, reroute me via London, where my layover would be eleven hours. I took the option, and for the inconvenience caused by my flight delays, the representative was kind enough to bump me up to business class. For many of you traveling business class might be ordinary, but for me this was a new experience, which included priority boarding, bigger and reclining seats in the front section of the plane, wonderful food and a wide selection of drinks, served on china and in real glasses. The best part of this experience was the business class lounge at Heathrow airport, replete with showers, gourmet foods, internet use, even massage chairs. This was a completely different world from the world that I was used to—the world of crowded terminals, loud, unending announcements, tired-looking passengers wheeling their heavy carry-on bags, and tasteless but very expensive food! Honestly, I had no idea that spaces such as the business class lounge existed in the world of airports!

Reconciliation involves a similar invitation to step into and experience a fresh new world. In this connection, reconciliation is at the heart of Gospel. Paul more than any other New Testament authors captures the reality of the Gospel as the proclamation and invitation into this new world, which Paul also refers to as "new creation." For Paul, the death and resurrection of Christ has inaugurated a new reality and with it a new set of relationships and possibilities, where the old order as we know it has passed away, and the new one is here. No passage in the New Testament captures this reality as clearly as 2 Corinthians 5:17–20, where Paul explicitly connects the gift of new creation with the notion of reconciliation.[2] To the Corinthians, Paul writes:

> Therefore, if anyone is in Christ, the new creation has come. The old has gone, the new is here! All this is from God, who reconciled us to himself through Christ and gave us the ministry of reconciliation, that God was reconciling the world to himself in Christ, not counting people's sins against them. And he has committed to us the message of

---

[2] "Reconciliation" is a favorite Pauline term, occurring at least sixteen times within the Pauline corpus. See Murray J. Harris, *The Second Epistle to the Corinthians: A Commentary on the Greek Text* (Grand Rapids, MI: Eerdmans, 2005), 435.

reconciliation. We are therefore Christ's ambassadors, as though God were making his appeal through us. (NIV)

This is a rich text that calls for extensive hermeneutical and exegetical commentary, which time and space does not allow here. However, a number of observations are in order:

First, the central idea that what Paul is describing in this passage is not "reconciliation," but the "New Creation": "Therefore, if anyone is in Christ, the new creation has come. The old has gone, the new is here!" (v. 17). A number of New Testament scholars note that most translations of the original Greek text do not get it right and are thus misleading, especially when the text is translated (as ESV): "Therefore, if anyone is in Christ, he is a new creation." The translation is misleading because Paul is not talking about a personal state of salvation, but a cosmic reality. He is, in fact, not even describing this cosmic reality, but announcing it, with a kind of exhilaration. He is saying something like: "Anyone in Christ, there is a NEW CREATION!—the old is gone, the new is here!"[3]

Second, Paul announces as a matter of historical fact that "the old is gone, the new is here." He uses the word *pararchomai* "pass away." It is the same *pararchomai* that Paul explains in the letter to the Colossians as the passing away of the old man and the putting on of a new self (Col 3:10), and as the reality of (the believer) being irreversibly transferred ("rescued") from the kingdom of darkness into the kingdom of light, the kingdom of God's beloved son (Col 1:13). In all these usages, the *pararchomai*, the passing away, is described not simply as a metaphor, but as an actual (real) historical event that has taken place.

Third, the "new creation" is a gift. All this, Paul declares, "is from God."

Fourth, it is within this context of announcing, indeed celebrat-

---

[3] For a comprehensive discussion of the notion of New Creation in Paul, see T. Ryan Jackson, *New Creation in Paul's Letters: A Study of the Historical and Social Setting of a Pauline Concept*, Wissenschaftliche Untersuchungen zum Neuen Testament, 2 Reihe (2010; Eugene, OR: Wipf and Stock, 2016). See also Richard B. Hays, *The Moral Vision of the New Testament: Community, Cross, New Creation: A Contemporary Introduction to New Testament Ethics* (San Francisco: HarperSanFrancisco, 1996).

ing the New Creation that Paul uses the term "reconciliation" (five times in this short passage) as the process through which the *pararchomai* of the old order and the inauguration of the new creation has been effected: "God in Christ was reconciling the world." The Greek word *katalasso* (and its derivative *katalagge* that Paul also uses) is not a religious term. Paul borrows the word from the political and legal sphere, where the word was used to mean an "exchange of one thing for another." Within this context, what Paul is saying is that the new creation has been realized: through *katalagge*—a kind of exchange of the old with the new—the exchange of enmity for friendship, a reordering of the relationships that had been disrupted, or the reestablishment of an equilibrium that had been lost.

Fifth, the exchange does not simply transform human beings; the exchange is cosmic: "God was reconciling the world [*kosmos*]." The scope of God's action of restoration is not simply personal. The entire created order (personal, social, ecological, economic, political) has been renewed—thus a New Creation, where "all things [are] reconciled in Christ" (Col 1:20). The Old Testament equivalent of what Paul has in mind here is "shalom."

Sixth, at the heart of this movement of restoration is that it is realized "in Christ"—en Christo. This is Paul's favorite expression, which occurs more than 160 times in the Pauline corpus and five times in this short passage.[4] The reason behind this "unifying motif in Pauline Theology" is that for Paul the Christ event is a decisive moment in God's relationship and journey with creation. If God "has been reconciling the world" in Christ, that effort comes to an ultimate realization. The effect is that in Christ, God's new creation becomes visible, but also that Christ's Lordship of God's creation comes to be uniquely revealed in Christ's passion, death, and resurrection. Thus, Paul's hymn (rhapsody) in Colossians 1:15–20:

> The Son is the image of the invisible God, the firstborn over all creation. For in him all things were created: things in heaven and on earth, visible and invisible, whether thrones or powers or rulers or authorities; all things have been

---

[4]Harris, *Second Epistle to the Corinthians*, 431.

created through him and for him. He is before all things, and in him all things hold together. And he is the head of the body, the church; he is the beginning and the firstborn from among the dead, so that in everything he might have the supremacy. For God was pleased to have all his fullness dwell in him, and through him to reconcile to himself all things, whether things on earth or things in heaven, by making peace through his blood, shed on the cross.

What becomes obvious from this short commentary is that the major themes of Paul's theology (new creation, reconciliation, the Christ event, grace, the gift) are all captured in the passage of 2 Corinthians 5:17–20. This passage serves as a kind of summary of the Good News—of the Gospel as Paul understood it. That Good News is not merely a spiritual atonement or cleansing of a sinner's guilt, but a total reordering of creation, an exchange of an old order of things, and the inauguration of a new dispensation. Reconciliation is the process through which the restoring of a broken creation is realized by God.

How Then Shall We Live?

The question then becomes how should "anyone in Christ" live in view of this Good News of the new creation made possible through God's reconciling work? Three immediate implications stand out.

The Gift: All This Is from God

As noted, the immediate context for Paul's use of the notion of reconciliation in the passage above is to announce—nay, celebrate—the gift of new creation. "All this is from God," Paul notes. Reconciliation thus invokes *gratitude* as the Christian's primary posture and attitude in life. For many people this posture is difficult to sustain not only in the face of personal challenges of sickness, sin, broken relationships, poverty, discrimination (you name it), but in the face of all sorts of injustice, violence, poverty, terrorism, and evil structures in the world. Although these realities are real, Paul's proclamation of new creation is an invitation for

Christians to stand within and experience another realism within which their lives have been drawn, not simply in a spiritual or metaphorical sense, but in reality—as a matter of fact. That is why the primary gift connected with reconciliation has to do with how we see the world. How we see the world makes all the difference in how we live in the world, for we can only act in the world according to how we see it. In the verse immediately before Paul announces "new creation," he reminds the Corinthians: "So from now on we regard no one from a worldly point of view. Though we once regarded Christ in this way, we do so no longer" (v. 16). What this means is that the gift of reconciliation is the gift of a new lens—a new way of seeing the world: the world not only as the theater of God's reconciling work, but the world as already healed (the old is gone, the new is here). But the fact that "all this is from God" makes the Christian life one of constant anticipation, reception, and gratitude for God's healing that is always going on, both in one's personal life and in the world.

Ambassadors: Christians as Resident Aliens

In the exhortation concluding the passage of 2 Corinthians 5: 17–20, Paul tells the Corinthians: "The message [*diakonia*—service] has been entrusted to us. We are therefore Christ's ambassadors." In Paul's time, ambassadors (*presbeuo,* singular *presbus*) were usually older experienced men, who acted as representatives or legates of the ruling authority in another town or city.[5] In using the image of an ambassador, Paul is inviting the Christians to live as resident aliens[6] and see their lives in the world as a kind of diplomatic posting. For even as Paul announced the new creation as a matter of historical fact, as a reality that has already happened in Christ, and as the dominion under which anyone in Christ is

---

[5]That Paul uses another image (*presbeuo*) drawn from the political sphere is quite telling. Just as with *Katalasso, presbeuo* confirms the political overtones of the new creation. One must, however, not understand "political" here in terms of narrow partisan politics—but as something connected to everyday activities in the world (as opposed to the narrow "spiritual" sense).

[6]For an extended discussion of the notion of "resident aliens" from which I am drawing, see Stanley Hauerwas and William H. Willimon, *Resident Aliens: Life in the Christian Colony* (Nashville, TN: Abingdon, 2014).

placed, he was well aware that the Christian continued to live in the world of old creation with all its stubborn patterns of sin, war, injustice, poverty, racism, discrimination, and selfishness. Like a good ambassador, the Christian needs to learn and understand the operations of this world, the language and way of life of the locations of the posting, participate in its life, enjoy some of the gifts the country offers, including culture, food, and friendships. And yet even as the ambassador does so, he or she cannot lose sight of, or forget the policies, objectives, strategic directions, and ambitions of his or her original country, whose interests the ambassador represents and advocates for. The practical import of this observation is that the Christians always find themselves in that "in-between," the already and not yet of the new creation, between the now and the final realization of God's new creation when all Christians will be subject to Christ's dominion. For as Paul notes in Romans: the entire creation is groaning, waiting for the full liberation of God's children (Rom 8:19–22). To sustain life in that in-between requires that at all times, Christians keep their feet on the ground and their eyes in the clouds.[7]

The Journey of Reconciliation: Feet on the Ground and Eyes in the Clouds

Living in the already and not yet of God's new creation, the Christian experiences reconciliation both as a gift (to be received) and as something to be realized through effort. For this reason, even as Christian life is grounded in gratitude and thanksgiving (God has reconciled the world), it is also a life of straining and endless advocacy against the structures of sin, injustice, poverty, and hatred that resist the full liberation of God's children. The fact that the full realization of God's new creation will never be realized this side of the Parousia means that healing will always be experienced as incomplete, broken, and piecemeal. This is to say that reconciliation is not an event, but a journey, which is experienced as liberating, but also agonizing, and quite often frustrating. At least five disciplines are necessary if the Christian

---

[7]John Paul Lederach, *Reconcile: Conflict Transformation for Ordinary Christians* (Harrisonburg, VA: Herald Press, 2014), 23.

is to sustain this journey. These disciplines help Christians keep their feet on the ground and their eyes in the clouds.

1. Memory. To sustain the journey of reconciliation, the Christian must constantly remember the drama within which his or her concrete life here and now is located. The short form of the drama is: "God has been reconciling the world to Godself." In shaping Christian memory, the biblical story provides a sense not only of the "beginning" (creation) of God's journey with creation, the various stages of that journey: creation, the life of Israel, the climax in the Christ event, its ongoing manifestation in the life of the church as it moves forward toward its final realization of the new heaven and the new earth of Revelation. Without the memory shaped around the biblical story, it not only easy to lose sight of the end (telos) to which one's various struggles in the world are directed; one's imagination in relation to concrete possibilities and opportunities to advance God's new creation in the world becomes diminished.

2. Lament. Lament is about learning to see clearly, name rightly, and keep one's feet on the ground of pain without surrendering either to despair or to easy consolation. To lament is to learn to tell the truth of the brokenness in and around us. Doing so, however, can very easily be overwhelming because the realities of sin, injustice, suffering, pain, and selfishness are real and are never fully overcome. Lament is what helps the Christian live in the sluggish between. It is an invitation to see and feel what God sees and feels for God's broken creation. Locating the brokenness of the world within the story of God's own anguish helps one see and name truthfully what is going on. For without such truth, the temptation is to "heal lightly" the brokenness of the world, saying, as Jeremiah warns us, "peace, peace, when there is no peace" (Jer 6:14). For this reason, lament is an integral dimension of hope.

3. Hope. Hope is what helps keep lament from turning into despair. Faith, as the letter to the Hebrews notes, "is the evidence of things not seen" (11:1). It is hope that grounds the Christian journey in the firm conviction that even in the midst of the world's darkest history, God continues to sow seeds of a "new thing" (Is 43:19). Thus, hope is the commitment to live not simply with the realism of what is possible now, but with the madness of dreams drawn from a future yet to be seen. For this reason, hope locates the Christian in the company of "the cloud of witnesses" that extends from Abraham, Sarah, and Moses (Heb 11–12) to contemporary witnesses such as Martin Luther King Jr., Dorothy Day, Christophe Munzihirwa, Emmanuel Kataliko, and others who have lived with the evidence of things not seen. Surrounded by such a cloud of witnesses, not only is fear transformed into courage, but the Christian imagination of what is concretely possible is invigorated.

4. *Advocacy*. Hope is not an abstract reality. For as Augustine says, hope has two daughters: anger and courage. The anger at the way things are and the courage to see that they do not remain as they are. It is especially in relation to this discipline that the life of an ambassador provides a particularly poignant model. On a given day the issues the ambassador confronts are numerous. Moreover, although the ambassador may have guidelines, he or she often has no blueprint of how to go about the job. Just like an ambassador, the Christian must learn to view his or her life in the world not in terms of a given from which he or she dare not deviate, but rather as a series of engagements, with a number of gifts and challenges which he or she can accept and transform into opportunities within the drama of God's story of love for the world. Accordingly, just like an ambassador, the skill that the Christian needs perhaps more than any other to live fully well into his or her status as "resident alien" and in the role as ambassador, is one of improvisation.[8] Advocacy is formed in the various opportunities for improvising hope in the world.

5. *Intimacy*. Even as the journey of reconciliation is about the endless advocacy for peace, justice, human rights, and an end to war and violence in the world, it is a deeply personal journey. Our own lives are broken, and the gift of reconciliation gets constantly tested by the people closest to us who are often times the most difficult to love. Moreover, reconciliation calls us into the hard spaces between the already and the not yet. The questions "Why me?" and "Why go on?" will constantly confront us at critical times when the cost is high, forgiveness too painful, the hurt too deep, and the resistance too strong. All said, the journey of

---

[8] For a full explication of the notion of improvisation, see Samuel Wells, *Improvisation: The Drama of Christian Ethics* (Grand Rapids, MI: Brazos Press, 2004).

reconciliation is a journey of being drawn closer to Christ, who, we are reminded, "for the sake of the joy that was set before him, endured the cross" (Heb 12:2). For this reason the journey involves and requires moments of prayer, silence, and devotion, which nurture intimacy with God and build up spiritual resources to sustain the journey for the long haul.

The Sacrament of Our Reconciliation

Within the context of the Christian life as a journey of reconciliation, Christian worship, the Mass in particular, takes on a special significance as both a school of formation and a "fueling station." First, in terms of formation, when Christians participate in the Eucharist, they are drawn into the drama of God's reconciliation. For instance, in the reading of scripture, the Preface, Eucharistic prayers, and other parts of the Mass, the memory of God's journey with creation is shaped, not simply as a remembrance of what happened, but as a reenactment of that story in time. Thus, just as my invitation into the world of business travel introduced me to something I had no idea existed, the sacramental life of the church invites Christians into and offers them an opportunity to actually stand within, feel, and experience that drama concretely both in its personal and social dimension. In this regard, the Mass becomes not simply a dress rehearsal for the real drama, which will happen outside the liturgy. The Mass is itself the drama of reconciliation—the "sacrament of our reconciliation" as we pray in the third Eucharistic prayer.[9] As a sacrament, it makes real both the journey and the patterns of memory, lament, hope, advocacy, and intimacy with God, which constitute that journey. The Mass thus locates Christians within and forms them in the habits of living in the now and not yet of new creation. In this connection, it is instructive that the shape of the Mass itself keeps moving back and forth between the past and the future; between what God has done, and what is yet to come; between remembrance (the night he was betrayed) and the anticipation for when "he comes again," between praise and petition, doxology and lament.

---

[9] "May this Sacrifice of our reconciliation, we pray, O Lord, advance the peace and salvation of all the world."

Second, in locating and holding Christians within dynamic tension between the already and the not yet, the Mass forms and reproduces in the life of the Christian an intimate connection between the healing that has already been experienced and the recalcitrant reality of sin, between hope and lament. At Mass, hope and lament go hand in hand—the rite of penance and the rite of communion intimately belong together, not simply as one being a condition for the other, but as the truth of our lives, namely that "while we were still sinners, Christ died for us" (Rom 5:6–8). And it is while we were sinners that—on the night before he died—he invited us to his table. The Eucharistic celebration thus invites us to see and experience the nature of the hope of Christian reconciliation, but also to realize that naming the truth of our sinfulness is a true sign of what it means to live in hope. Thus through penance and the confession of sins, we stand before God's judgment. But the reason we are not afraid to do so is because we are assured that God has already reconciled us—not counting our sins against us, a truth that the Eucharist communion confirms.

Third, the dynamic interaction between lament and hope helps keep the Christian grounded but also energized for the Christian journey. A story might not only provide a concrete illustration, it will help bring this presentation to a good conclusion. John Baptist Odama was installed as archbishop of Gulu diocese, in Northern Uganda, in 1999, where from 1986 until recently a group calling itself the Lord's Resistance Army waged war against the Ugandan government, terrorized the civilian population, burned villages, killed and maimed civilians, and abducted over 23,000 children as a means of recruitment into their fighting ranks. Odama became a fierce critic of the war, moving back and forth between Kony's fighters and the Museveni government seeking to mediate an end to hostilities, building a coalition of cultural and religious leaders (ARLPI), and joining the children to sleep on the streets of Gulu, thereby drawing international attention to the plight of the little ones. Asked what kept him going through the years of war and fueled his endless advocacy on behalf of the local population, Odama noted that it was the practice of setting aside Thursday and spending the entire day in prayer, fasting, and meditation before the Blessed Sacrament. Asked by a student what he did the entire day in front of the Blessed Sacrament, he said that he read scripture, confessed his sins, brought the names and faces of the children before God, named the gifts of the week, and prayed for the people.

That is what the journey of reconciliation is about: allowing the story of God's new creation to shape one's vision and involvement in the world. Christian worship, the Mass in particular, allows the Christian to step into that drama, relive it and keep one's eyes on the gift, invitation, and telos of the journey. Thus, rather than absolving the Christian from attending to the brokenness of the world, the celebration of the Eucharist intensifies the attention to the world by forming the Christian into the vision and patterns of the new creation in the world.

2

Reconciling Justice

Transitional Justice, Radical Forgiveness,
and the Reinvention of Nation-State Politics
in Africa

Over the last decade or so, there has been a growing interest in what has come to be known as "transitional justice mechanisms." The interest has been shaped at the intersection of peace studies as a rapidly growing field of academic specialization, on the one hand, and on the other, of advocacy centers such as the International Center for Transitional Justice (ICTJ) and the African Transitional Justice Research Network. While scholars and researchers in peace studies have helped broaden scholarly debate on justice beyond a narrow focus on criminal justice into a more broad field of political justice, advocacy centers such as the ICTJ, based in New York, have sought to deliver, through advocacy, training, and other avenues, "technical expertise and knowledge" to institutions and civil society groups, to help in the implementation and monitoring of transitional justice mechanisms.[1]

This essay began as a lecture delivered as part of the Annual Justice Lecture Series, Eastern Mennonite University, Virginia, November 10, 2009.

[1]Based in New York, the International Center for Transitional Justice has branches all over the world, including eight in Africa. Its stated mission is "to redress and prevent the most severe violations of human rights by confronting legacies of mass abuse. ICTJ seeks holistic solutions to promote accountability and create just and peaceful societies." http://www.ictj.org. On its part, the African

The concept of transitional justice is relatively recent and can be traced back to the post–Second World War period in Europe with the establishment of the International Military Tribunal at Nuremberg and the various denazification programs in Germany and the trials of Japanese soldiers for crimes committed during the war. The concept has grown to now include judicial and non-judicial processes associated with a society's attempt to come to terms with a legacy of large-scale past abuses, in order to ensure accountability, serve justice, and achieve reconciliation.

Thus in its broad definition "transitional justice" refers to the "range of measures which might include criminal prosecutions, truth commissions, reparation programs, and various kinds of institutional reforms that societies undertake to reckon with the legacies of widespread or systematic human rights abuse as they move from a period of violent conflict or oppression towards peace, democracy, the rule of law and respect for human rights."[2]

A quick survey confirms that interest in transitional justice mechanisms is high in Africa. Following two coups d'état and a civil war, an independent commission of inquiry into human rights abuse was established in Côte d'Ivoire. In Burundi, an international commission of inquiry was established to investigate the assassination of President Mechior Ndadaye, and the massacres and other serious offenses committed between October 1993 and August 1995. Also, The Arusha Accord on peace and reconciliation in Burundi, signed in August 2000, called for the establishment of a truth and reconciliation commission (TRC) as well as an international judicial commission of inquiry. In December 2004 the Burundian Parliament passed a law establishing a TRC. Following the Arusha Peace Accord of 2000, the ICTJ has advised the Burundi government on a number of consultative,

---

Transition Justice Research Network, based in South Africa, has as its stated mission: "to promote and encourage transitional justice research in Africa through the development of research capacity, the building of transitional justice content knowledge, and the creation of spaces for practitioners and researchers in Africa to share experiences, expertise, and lessons learned. The goal is to ensure that the transitional justice agenda in Africa is locally informed and owned" (http://www.transitionaljustice.org).

[2]Charles Mango Fombad, "Transitional Justice in Africa: The Experience with Truth Commissions," Hauser Global Law School Program, *GlobaLex* (May/June 2008), http://www.nyulawglobal.org.

participatory, and victim-centered transitional justice strategies. In Kenya, the intense violence and political unrest that threatened to destabilize Kenya following its contested presidential elections in late December 2007 led to a round of negotiations beginning in late January 2008, known as the Kenya National Dialogue and Reconciliation. Brokered by the African Union's Panel of Eminent African Personalities, which is chaired by former UN Secretary-General Kofi Annan. The negotiations produced terms for a grand coalition government including Mwai Kibaki's Party of National Unity (PNU) and Raila Odinga's Orange Democratic Movement. The accord led to the cessation of most violence and called for the establishment of several bodies of inquiry. These included a Commission of Inquiry on Post-election Violence (CIPEV), a Truth, Justice, and Reconciliation Commission (TJRC), and an Independent Review Committee (IREC) to investigate all aspects of the 2007 elections. In Liberia, with the departure of former president Charles Taylor and the conclusion of a Comprehensive Peace Agreement (CPA) in Accra, Ghana, in August 2003, the CPA mandated the creation of a national Truth and Reconciliation Commission (TRC), which was passed into law by the National Transitional Legislative Assembly in June 2005. In Sierra Leone, the ten-year civil war (1991–2002) was characterized by intense and cruel violence against civilians and the recruitment of child soldiers. The war claimed tens of thousands of civilian lives, and the number of persons raped, mutilated, or tortured is much higher. In July 1999, the government of Sierra Leone and the Revolutionary United Front (RUF) rebel group signed the Lomé Peace Agreement (LPA), which granted amnesty for all parties, even as it established a Truth and Reconciliation Commission (TRC).

These examples represent just a small sample. A more comprehensive survey will confirm that in the last twenty years, at least more than a third of the countries in Africa have attempted to address human rights abuses of their violent past by relying on a varied mix of transitional justice mechanisms, such as prosecutions, truth commissions, and reconciliation efforts. But this sheer number of African countries that have instituted one or a number of transitional justice mechanisms raises critical questions. First, how effective are transitional justice mechanisms that are meant to ensure truth, accountability, and the redress of past abuses? Second, how adequate is the notion of political justice as the primary lens for repairing societies rent apart by war and violence? These are serious *technical* questions that political scientists and policy makers need to address. My questions are of a different order; they are meta-technical or metaphysical questions regarding the nature and foundations of African politics. Why do so many African countries require transitional justice mechanisms? What is going on?

Second, transitional justice mechanisms are premised on the notion of transition from a violent past to a future of peace. Why does it seem that African countries are always transitioning into a democratic dispensation but never seem to ever get there? Third, what does the preponderance of transitional justice mechanisms reveal about the foundations of modern political life in Africa? Might this point to the fact that war, political impunity, and large-scale abuse of human rights are standard features of Africa's political life? If that is the case, then what needs to be addressed, beyond any particular national crisis, is the underlying imagination that makes violence an inevitable feature of modern Africa's political history. If this is the case, then theology might discover it has something significant to contribute to Africa's political future. My concern is that without seeking to reinvent Africa's social imaginary, transitional justice mechanisms simply turn into another form (the latest iteration) of firefighting mechanisms meant to prop up Africa's questionable political modernity.

Propping Up Africa's Political Modernity

Social or political ethics is popular in Africa. Many advocacy centers and institutions of higher learning offer courses and programs in good governance, human rights, development, and peace studies. One common element within these programs is the recognition that Africa's enduring social problems are somehow connected to the institution of the nation-state and its politics. Accordingly, both the theoretical and practical training offered through these various programs focus on ways to reform the function of nation-state politics in Africa, with the hope that once the nation-state becomes more functional and more democratic then peace and development will ensue. This is what makes social ethics highly popular, but also essentially prescriptive and pragmatic, with the various programs offering packaged "solutions" (often coming from the West) on how to "fix" Africa's political dysfunctionality. The technical solutions include how to have a free and fair election, how to monitor elections, and how to carry out constitutional reform and economic reform. In addition to these they include advocacy and a host of other recommendations to ensure good governance, accountability, and transparency.

In many ways, transitional justice mechanisms can be seen as yet another (latest iteration) of the efforts to help African nation-state politics work, grounded in the valid realization of the ongoing legacies of war and widespread abuse of human rights in Africa's postcolonial history. And like the previous prescriptions, transitional justice mechanisms are driven by a sense of optimism that applying the right mechanisms, processes, and techniques will solve the problems of politics in Africa. Transitional justice mechanisms are thus offered as the most effective way for African societies that have been marked by a history of violent conflict and human rights abuses to transition into a future of peace and democratic accountability. As Charles Monga Fombad notes in relation to truth commissions:

> It cannot be denied that truth commissions today provide the most viable, flexible and credible mechanism for laying down the foundations of a democratic society in Africa as well as resolving the numerous open or latent conflicts. They provide an avenue for taming, balancing and recasting the anger and desire for revenge in a positive direction that can provide progress, development, peace and prosperity."[3]

Fombad's optimism about transitional justice mechanisms in general and truth commissions in particular must of course be read against the background of the frustration that the much touted decade of democratization in Africa (1990s) has not ushered in the anticipated African renaissance. On the contrary, there

---

[3]Fombad, "Transitional Justice in Africa." For more on truth commissions in Africa, see http://www.nyulawglobal.org.

has been a rise in civil wars and human rights abuse on a mass scale in a number of countries in Africa: from the genocide in Rwanda to the brutal civil wars in Liberia, Sierra Leone, Southern Sudan, Northern Uganda, and Ivory Coast. These and similar experiences of political violence have left politicians, political theorists, and policy makers searching for mechanisms to help societies transition from a violent past into a future of peace. Another significant factor behind the optimism in relation to transitional justice mechanisms is the is the positive experience of the Truth and Reconciliation Commission in South Africa. For all its limitations, the TRC was successful in enabling South Africa to transition from an oppressive apartheid legacy into a democratic rainbow nation. This South African miracle[4] has inspired other African countries that hoped to move from years of similar history of oppression and repression to a democratic future. In the wake of South Africa's TRC, not only did interest in transitional justice mechanisms grow, but "reconciliation" became a standard feature of these mechanisms, as a number of countries sought to apply South Africa's model in their own countries. Thus the National Unity and Reconciliation Commission in Rwanda (1999); the National Reconciliation Commission in Ghana (2002); the Truth, Justice, and Reconciliation Commission in Kenya (2003); the Commission Verité et Réconciliation in Congo (2004); the Equality and Reconciliation Commission in Morocco (2004); the Truth and Reconciliation Commission in Liberia (2005); and the Truth, Justice and Reconciliation Commission in Togo (2009) were all established.

Another significant observation that may help explain the optimism (of Fombad and others) that transitional justice mechanisms may provide "the most viable, flexible and credible mechanism for laying down the foundations of a democratic society in Africa" has to do with the perceived congruence between some of the transitional justice mechanisms with African cultural values and with African indigenous justice systems. For many, including Desmond Tutu, one reason behind the success of the TRC was that it was grounded in the African concept of *Ubuntu*, or

---

[4]For a good discussion of the TRC as both model and miracle, see Lyn S. Graybill, *Truth and Reconciliation in South Africa: Miracle or Model?* (Boulder, CO: Lynne Rienner, 2002).

humanness, which encourages forgiveness and the restoration of the offender.[5] It was with a similar appeal to African cultural wisdom and indigenous justice systems that Rwanda, in the aftermath of the genocide, instituted the *gacaca* courts (2005), a combination of truth finding and prosecuting mechanisms that operated in precolonial Rwanda. The mandate of the *gacaca* was to bring about justice and reconciliation at the grassroots level, which included the restoration of forgiven perpetrators back into the community. In a similar vein, a number of religious and civil society activists in Northern Uganda criticized the indictments (2005) of Joseph Kony and other leaders of the Lord's Resistance Army (LRA) by the International Criminal Court (ICC), opting instead for a combination of amnesty and the traditional practice of *Mato Oput* (drinking the bitter herb), which involves reconciliation between communities and the reintegration of the offender into the community.

It must be noted that positively, the various transitional justice mechanisms attempt to respond to the serious challenge of violence and the legacies of widespread abuse of human rights. Moreover, what the discourse on transitional justice, especially the appeal to African cultural notions and indigenous justice systems, has helped to do is to broaden the discussion of justice beyond the usual discussion of retributive justice to a richer notion of restorative justice. It is, however, a long shot from acknowledging this positive contribution of transitional justice mechanisms to the claim that they are the "most viable, flexible and credible mechanism for laying down the foundations of a democratic society in Africa as well as resolving the numerous open or latent conflicts." For structurally, there does not seem to be any difference between the various transitional justice mechanisms than other solutions that have been prescribed to help fix the dysfunctionality of the African nation-state politics. Even the appeal to African cultural values and practices is often nothing more than an attempt to provide cultural legitimation or find usable insights from the

---

[5] John Allen, *Rabble-Rouser for Peace: The Authorized Biography of Desmond Tutu* (Chicago: Lawrence Hill Books, 2008): 347. For a critical view on this, see Christian B. N. Gade, "Restorative Justice and the South African Truth and Reconciliation Process," *South African Journal of Philosophy* 32, no. 1 (2013): 10–35.

African past to carry forward the modern project.[6] None of the attempts, however, question the problematic foundations of Africa's political modernity, which is grounded in an imagination of violence, and thus reproduces violence as an ongoing feature of nation-state politics in Africa. Without questioning the imaginary of nation-state politics, transitional justice mechanisms become just another form of firefighting in the ongoing melodrama of political violence in Africa. The critical point we are making here can be made more explicit by highlighting three critical issues connected to transitional justice mechanisms.

When Justice Is Not Enough: Critical Questions

Expecting Too Much

The first critical issue has to do with the optimism surrounding transitional justice mechanisms, which I have already alluded to. The case of the Democratic Republic of the Congo is particularly illuminating. The Commission Verité et Réconciliation (CVR) was established as one of the five institutions in support of a democratic transition encompassed in the Pretoria power-sharing

---

[6]The appeal to religion works in the same way. That is why the notion of "reconciliation"—a notion so capacious that it could mean anything—can be a tantalizing temptation for Christian social ethics. For while, on the one hand, given its religious connotation, it can be a confirmation of how religion in general, Christianity in particular, can be useful in the nation-building project, the appeal to reconciliation focuses only on what is usable about reconciliation for the nation-state political project, but does engage reconciliation in its full theo-political dimensions. Dan Philpott, my colleague at the University of Notre Dame has made a case for political reconciliation as a concept of justice, mercy, and peace that is rooted in the religious tradition of Christianity, Judaism, and Islam, which can provide societies dealing with legacies of political injustice and widespread violations of human rights with a possibility to transition into a future of peace (Daniel Philpott, *Just and Unjust Peace: An Ethic of Political Reconciliation* [Oxford: Oxford University Press 2012]). There is a lot I find helpful in Philpott's argument. However, his case for restorative justice rooted in the religious logic of reconciliation is based on a selective reading of religious tradition in order to find the "overlapping consensus" he needs to portray the usefulness of the religious traditions and how they can positively contribute to modern political project. He does not consider how "reconciliation," if read from within the context of the religious tradition, could offer visions of well-being that might be at odds with some dimensions of the modern political agenda and might in other cases even call into question the "peace" of secular democratic institutions.

agreement, which was signed in December 2002. The mandate of the commission was to "reestablish truth and promote peace, justice, reparation, forgiveness and reconciliation, with the view of consolidating national unity." The commission was also responsible for investigating political crimes and human rights violations which took place from June 30, 1960, to the end of the transition.[7]

In the first place, one wonders how a single commission could be expected to realize such a wide-ranging set of expectations, including establishing truth, dealing with historical memory, investigating political crimes and human rights violations, delivering justice, achieving reconciliation, consolidating national unity, and ensuring forgiveness and reparation. The question I raise in relation to the CVR can be raised, *mutatis mutandis*, about other transitional justice programs, including the Gacaca in Rwanda. To expect that one commission would be able to deliver all that is to expect too much. And the problem is not simply one of logistical challenge, but points to the vast sociopolitical and institutional lacunae that transitional justice mechanisms are supposed to fill.

Transition to What?

The same point can be raised from another angle. As already noted, transitional justice mechanisms are often described as approaches that societies "undertake to reckon with the legacies of widespread or systematic human rights abuse as they move from a period of violent conflict or oppression toward peace, democracy, the rule of law and respect for human rights."[8]

If the case of the Congo is anything to go by, there is a lot to question about the expectation of "transition." No doubt there was much optimism and anticipation of a new day in the DRC following the 2012 Pretoria agreement that established the CRV. As part of the agreement Rwanda agreed to the withdrawal of the estimated 20,000 Rwandan troops from the DRC in exchange for an international commitment toward the disarmament of the Hutu militia *interahamwe* and ex-FAR (Rwandan Armed Forces)

---

[7]Fombad, "Transitional Justice in Africa," 5.
[8]Ibid.

fighters. The agreement also paved the way for the transition government headed by President Joseph Kabila, the new constitution, and the 2006 general elections, which Joseph Kabila won. On one hand, one might look at these positive developments as indications of transition into a more democratic future. But anyone familiar with the developments in the Congo realizes that there has been no such transition. First, since 2015 President Joseph Kabila has been desperately trying to change the constitution to allow him to run again, beyond the constitutional limits. Hundreds of people have been killed in the demonstrations opposing the president. Second, the anticipated peace and end to fighting never happened. On the contrary, the country, especially Eastern Congo, has continued to experience violent conflicts and militia violence that have left over 3.4 million people dead, tens of thousands of women raped, and millions displaced from their homes.[9] Although the case of the Congo may seem like an exception, in many ways it provides a useful lens into much of sub-Saharan Africa,[10] which leads one to wonder whether violence is simply part of the political imaginary of modern Africa.

Violence as "Exception"

Part of the optimism connected to transitional justice mechanisms is the assumption that human rights abuse, violence, and civil unrest are exceptions to the normal functioning of nation-state politics.[11] This, however, is not the case, certainly not in

---

[9]See Jason K. Stearns, *Dancing in the Glory of Monsters: The Collapse of the Congo and the Great War of Africa* (New York: Public Affairs, 2012).

[10]Thus the image of Congo as a mirror—or to use Frantz Fanon's famous image: Africa has the shape of a pistol, and Congo is the trigger (Stearns, *Dancing in the Glory of Monsters*, 45). See also Michela Wrong, *In the Footsteps of Mr. Kurtz: Living on the Brink of Disaster in Mobutu's Congo* (New York: HarperCollins, 2001), 10.

[11]For an argument that violence is a feature of modern political life, both in the founding of the nation-state institution and its perpetuation, see Anthony Giddens, *The Nation-State and Violence*, vol. 2 *of A Contemporary Critique of Historical Materialism* (Berkeley: University of California Press, 1987). See also William T. Cavanaugh, *The Myth of Religious Violence: Secular Ideology and the Roots of Modern Conflict* (New York: Oxford University Press, 2009); Cavanaugh persuasively argues that contrary to the usual impression, the state is not a neutral actor and pacifier in the "wars of religion."

Africa. On the contrary, as scholars such as Patrick Chabal, Jean-Pascal Daloz, Mahmood Mamdani, and others have noted,[12] violence, chaos, and banditry are not an exception but part of the "normal" functioning of nation-state politics in Africa.[13] A similar point has been made more forcibly by Bill Berkeley in *The Graves Are Not Yet Full* in relation to Rwanda: "A widespread misconception of the post–cold war era is that ethnic conflict is a by-product of 'failed' states. Rwanda represents the opposite: a state—albeit criminal—that was all too successful in mobilizing along rigidly hierarchical lines from the top down, from the head of state and his ruling clique down to the last village mayor, making possible the slaughter, mostly with clubs and machetes, of hundreds of thousands in barely three months."[14] The combined effect of these observations is to confirm the Mamdani's conclusion that the Rwanda genocide is not an exception but a "*metaphor* for postcolonial political violence"[15] in Africa.

Rudolph Joseph Rummel, the late eminent professor of political science at University of Hawaii, points to a similar sobering conclusion when he notes that contrary to the usual assumption, more deaths in the twentieth century have been caused by the victims' own government than by war. War's visibility often distorts and obscures this fact.[16] Rummel does not specifically focus his observations on Africa, but his argument that death by government, or what he calls "democide," accounts for six times more deaths of its own citizens than war, rings true in many parts of Africa, and calls for pause in the optimism for a transition to democracy, peace, the rule of law, and the protection of human rights in Africa.

For, if we combine Rummel's observations with the insights of Berkeley, Mamdani, Chabal, and Daloz, then the obvious conclu-

---

[12] Mahmood Mamdani, *When Victims Become Killers: Colonialism, Nativism, and the Genocide in Rwanda* (Princeton, NJ: Princeton University Press, 2002); Patrick Chabal and Jean-Pascal Daloz, *Africa Works: Disorder as Political Instrument* (Bloomington: Indiana University Press, 1999).

[13] See my *The Sacrifice of Africa: A Political Theology for Africa* (Grand Rapids, MI: Eerdmans, 2011) for a full explication of this claim

[14] Bill Berkeley, *The Graves Are Not Yet Full: Race, Tribe, and Power in the Heart of Africa* (New York: Basic Books, 2002), 15.

[15] Mamdani, *When Victims Become Killers*, ix.

[16] R. J. Rummel, *Death by Government* (New Brunswick, NJ: Transaction, 1994).

sion is that political violence in Africa does not reflect failure or weakness of the state, but is somehow wired into the political imaginary of Africa's modernity. The force of this realization is to shift the conversation of politics in Africa from the preoccupation with technical solutions to make politics work to an engagement with the imaginary of nation-state politics in Africa. Such a shift will inevitably reveal that the most pressing challenge of African societies marked by mass violence and rampant abuse of human rights is not so much one of justice (or even transitional justice), but the reinvention of the visions, imaginations, and stories that sustain modern political life Africa.

It is such reinvention that is at stake in the radical interruption of forgiveness by Angelina Atyam, the co-founder of the Concerned Parents Association (CPA) in Northern Uganda. Her story illuminates the theo-political story of reconciliation that can make the reinvention of politics in Africa possible. Assumed in my telling of the story of Atyam are two crucial assumptions. First, since the social political imaginary is grounded in mythoi or stories that shape a society's institutions and history, reinventing Africa's social imaginary involves a concerted effort to ground political life in new stories that offer the possibility for a new future beyond the story of "fighting." Reconciliation is such a story. Second, the engagement with stories offers an opportunity for theological engagement of Africa's political life in a manner that the focus on technical processes does not. Accordingly, telling Atyam's story points to the shape and direction of that political theology needs to take in Africa.

Angelina Atyam: Reinventing Africa's Political Modernity

In 2004 the United Nations described the situation in Northern Uganda as the worst and most neglected humanitarian crisis.[17] By then the civil war in Northern Uganda, which had pitted the Lord's Resistance Army, a ragtag group of militias fighters led by Joseph Kony against the Uganda government, had been raging on for over eighteen years. Over 300,000 people had been

---

[17]United Nations, "UN Relief Official Spotlights World's Largest Neglected Crisis in Northern Uganda," October 21, 2004, http://www.un.org.

killed; millions were displaced from their homes; and over 26,000 children were abducted by the LRA.

In 1996 Angelina Atyam's daughter was abducted by the rebels of the Lord's Resistance Army.[18] Atyam used to meet with the other parents of the abducted girls to advocate, fast, and pray for the release of their daughters. As they concluded each meeting they would pray the Lord's Prayer, but were unable to get beyond the words "forgive us our trespasses as. . . ." They were filled with anger and bitterness for their daughters' captivity. At one such meeting, feeling convicted by the Lord's Prayer, Atyam admonished the other parents: "We are wasting our time. How can we pray for the release of our daughters if we have not learned to forgive them." After some time, the parents were able to say the Lord's Prayer in full. "The Lord's forgiveness had come over us, and with that we felt we were able to somehow forgive even the rebels." The parents also felt the need to share the newly found gift of forgiveness with others in the community. On her part, Angelina Atyam went to meet and extend forgiveness to the mother of the rebel commander who was keeping her daughter in the bush.

While the newly found gift of forgiveness was enabling Atyam and the other parents to extend forgiveness even to the rebels, it also deepened their advocacy for the release of their children. They formed an advocacy group, the Concerned Parents' Association (CPA), through which they advocated in the community and over the radio to the international community. They appealed to the rebels and the government to end the war and release all the abducted children. As Atyam spoke against the atrocities of the rebels on one of the radio shows, the rebel commanders called in and wished to meet with her. He offered her a deal. They would release her daughter if she would shut up—if she would stop her advocacy, which was drawing negative attention to them. Atyam responded that she would do so only if they released all the abducted children, because, she told the rebels, "every child is my child." She went back home without her daughter to continue advocacy for the return of all children and to end the fighting.

Needless to say, this was a difficult decision because she knew

---

[18]A full study and discussion of Angelina Atyam's politics of forgiveness is found in my *Sacrifice of Africa*, 148–65. Here I give just an outline that nevertheless is sufficient to capture the full political significance of her story of forgiveness.

the horror that her daughter was undergoing as a sex slave—a "wife" to a rebel commander. Atyam's family could not understand how she had come to "sacrifice" her own child! Angelina Atyam's response was "I could not do otherwise. . . . The other children too had become my children." She not only intensified her advocacy, she continued to pray for her daughter and the other children, and to hope that one day God would allow for their release. Seven years into the abduction Angelina spent the night in prayer "arguing and wrestling" with God.

"The Bible says that you do not change," she asked God. "For seven years I have not seen my daughter, yet the Bible says the seventh year is a year of Jubilee and of release to the captives. Have you changed in my situation? When your son went to visit Martha and Mary, why did he cry at the death of Lazarus?" With these and similar questions, she assaulted God until she fell asleep at dawn. Three days later, she got a telephone call with the news that her daughter had escaped. She brought home two children that she had conceived in the bush, which Angelina Atyam renamed "God's Power" and "Miracle."

There are a number of aspects in Angelina Atyam's story that confirm the full extent and unique political character of her activism. First is the sense of journey it displays and how the journey points to a search for a new future in Northern Uganda that is not premised on fighting. Atyam's journey from bitterness to forgiveness to advocacy first for the return of her daughter and then for the return of all abducted children, and eventually for an end to all fighting reflects a deepening realization that, as she points out, "war cannot give us peace." It is within this logic that Atyam and the CPA, together with other religious and civil organizations, criticized the indictment of Kony by the ICC. Asked about her outspoken criticism of the ICC, Atyam noted: "We are tired of fighting. Kony is also our 'child,' even though a crazy and violent one. We want him to 'come home' and live with the mayhem he has created." Tim Allen is therefore wrong to suggest that all those opposed to the ICC indictment do so out of ignorance.[19] What Allen does not realize is that advocates such as

---

[19]The 2005 ICC indictments of Joseph Kony and other top members of the LRA were received with reservations and outright condemnation by a wide range of individuals and civic groups in Northern Uganda, which included Acholi

Angelina Atyam are not simply making a misinformed preference for cultural means of transitional justice or *Mato Oput* over the ICC, they are searching for a far deeper sense of justice: justice as peace, and for a different foundation of society—one that is not grounded in an economy of fighting. For what people like Atyam have come to realize, partly through their own bitter loss, is that that while people like Kony are a major obstacle to peace, simply apprehending them or trying them does not hold the key to a new postviolence future because Kony and his ilk are players within an underlying economy of violence that drives political life in Africa. It is this economy of violence that also explains the Uganda government's willingness to sacrifice millions in Northern Uganda in its determined effort to "crush" and "finish off" the LRA rebel fighters.

Second, Atyam's journey involves a search for a new community, one grounded in a different logic than the logic of power struggle and control that equally drives Kony's fighters and Museveni's army, whose effect is the wanton sacrifice of millions of innocent Ugandans. Atyam's journey of forgiveness and willingness to sacrifice her own daughter on behalf of "every child" reflects instead another logic, one that is grounded in the story of God's self-sacrificing love for humanity. If, following her daughter's abduction, the weekly meetings, prayers, fasting, and common advocacy were able to unite Atyam's painful journey with the journey of the other parents, thus forging a sense of community, the weekly practices, and more specifically the "Our Father" were significantly able to locate her story and that of the other parents into the broader story of God's self-sacrificing love. In this way, Atyam understands her willingness to sacrifice her own daughter as a participation in God's own sacrifice, which as René Girard would say is a "sacrifice to end all sacrifice."[20]

---

traditional leaders, representatives of the Christian churches, and NGOs. Tim Allen of the London School of Economics dismisses the reservations. He argues that much of the antipathy to the ICC is based on ignorance and misconception. Drawing on field research in Uganda, he comes to the conclusion that victims are much more interested in punitive international justice than has been suggested, and that the ICC has made resolution of the war more likely. See Tim Allen, *Trial Justice: The International Criminal Court and the Lord's Resistance Army* (London: Zed Books, 2006).

[20]According to René Girard, the scapegoat mechanism is the origin of sacrifice

The effect of this self-sacrificing love is a new community that extends beyond biological and ethnic boundaries and includes "every child." Formerly a midwife, Angelina Atyam's journey of forgiveness was not only able to explode her own sense of "who are my people" but turn her into a midwife for this new community that includes even Kony and the rebels.

Third, used as we are to a geographically bound, ethnically confined, and power-driven sense of politics, one, moreover, that accepts sacrificing others, particularly the weak, as necessary collateral damage, Atyam's politics of self-sacrificing love cannot but strike us as at once odd and utopian. This is the sentiment that was well captured by an elderly, blind woman whose only grandson had been abducted by the rebels. Listening to Atyam talk about extending forgiveness to the rebels, the elderly woman asked, "Angelina, are you from another planet?" The elderly woman is right. Atyam's forgiveness is indeed from another planet; it reflects another logic—God's way of redeeming, re-creating the world by "reconciling the world to himself in Christ, not counting people's sins against them" (2 Cor 5:19), and thus demonstrating his own love for us that "while we were still sinners, Christ died for us" (Rom 5:8). It is this "ontology of forgiveness"[21] that seeks not simply the repair of social space rent by violence, but the restoration

---

and the foundation of human culture. Religion was necessary in human evolution to control the violence that can come from mimetic rivalry. The revolutionary (and "'saving'") force of Christianity lies in the fact that Jesus, by offering himself on the cross, is able to break this cycle of violence-sacrifice. His death on the cross thus becoming the sacrifice to end all sacrifice. For an excellent discussion of this thesis, see Mark S. Heim, *Saved from Sacrifice: A Theology of the Cross* (Grand Rapids, MI: Eerdmans, 2006).

[21]Allan Torrance makes what I find to be a very helpful distinction between "an ethic of forgiveness" and an "ontology of forgiveness." Whereas an "'ethic of forgiveness" revolves around exhortations to forgive, an ontology of forgiveness points to the overarching framework that makes Christian forgiveness intelligible as a participation in the triune event of forgiveness. "Forgiveness," Torrance writes, "does not concern an abstruse, amorphous ethical principle or ideal with practical psychological or political relevance. Rather, it denotes concrete participation by grace in God's unconditional forgiveness of enemies that, to the extent they are ours, are also his but whom he also loves and forgives." Allan J. Torrance, "The Theological Grounds for Advocating Forgiveness and Reconciliation in the Sociopolitical Realm," in *The Politics of Past Evil: Religion, Reconciliation, and the Dilemmas of Transitional Justice,* ed. Dan Philpott (Notre Dame, IN: University of Notre Dame Press, 2006), 74, 76.

of all things, whether in heaven or on earth, unto God—which is to say according to their original purpose. This is the ontology within which Angelina Atyam stands and, like a true ambassador, seeks to invite others into its social and practical implications.

Finally, what role does justice play within this "ontology of forgiveness"? Does this mean that one has to completely dispense with the notion of transitional justice? Perhaps not, but what is clear from Atyam's story is that justice does not have the first word. On the contrary, from within the ontology of forgiveness, the very notion of justice is shown to be inadequate in dealing with what Hannah Arendt described as the "predicament of irreversibility."[22] "I do not know what justice would mean," Atyam admitted when pressed as to whether she would like to see justice for Kony. "Nothing will bring back the many people killed and the children lost. Only God can, and only God knows what to do with Kony." Atyam is not only pointing to the limits of "justice"; she recasts and subsumes the notion of justice under a theological vision—"only God can, and only God knows what to do with Kony." But in so doing she opens up the possibility of redirecting any considerations of justice to a specifically Christian telos. This is what makes her remarks particularly poignant. For since in scripture, at least in the New Testament, justice is associated with God's righteousness (*dikaiosune*), and the latter always has a connotation of restoration,[23] Atyam's hesitations about justice for Kony can only make sense in light of the story of God's redeeming and reconciling work. The sense of justice as redemption invoked by Atyam is even more explicitly captured by Archbishop John Baptist Odama, who, like Atyam was also critical of the ICC indictment of Kony. Asked about whether he would not like to see Kony brought to justice, Odama responded: "The question is not so much whether Kony should be brought

---

[22]Hannah Arendt, *The Human Condition: A Study of the Central Dilemmas Facing Modern Man* (Garden City, NY: Doubleday, 1959), 212ff. Evil acts, Arendt notes, cannot be undone. No one can undo what they have done. If they could be undone, then revenge simply would not be necessary. An immediate implication that Alan Torrance rightly draws from this observation is the failure of "justice" to deliver what it promises—to make things *iustus*, "right" (Torrance, "Theological Grounds for Advocating Forgiveness," 61).

[23]Christopher D. Marshall, *Beyond Retribution: A New Testament Vision for Justice, Crime, and Punishment* (Grand Rapids, MI: Eerdmans, 2001), 36–40.

to justice, but whether Kony can be saved." Pressed as to what salvation might mean for Kony, Odama answered, "Salvation is understanding; salvation is justice; salvation is 'welcome back'; salvation is feeling accepted. . . . The worst offense is to feel rejected; to feel that 'nobody is with me.'"[24]

Obviously, Angelina Atyam's story raises a number of questions, of which the relation between forgiveness and justice is an obvious one. Other questions might relate to its effectiveness in bringing the war in Northern Uganda to an end. What role would it play in repairing the wounds of war and ensuring a transition into a future of peace once the war has ended? What might be the relation between Christian forgiveness (practiced by Atyam) and the cultural practices of *Mato Oput*? How widespread might the sentiment or practice of forgiveness be? And how exactly does it work in a context of mass atrocity and widespread violence? Who forgives whom and on behalf of whom? Whereas these might be valid questions that need answers,[25] focusing on these questions here is to see in Atyam's story an exhortation for an ethic of forgiveness rather than pointing to an ontology—a different order and logic of society. My aim in introducing her story here has been primarily to shift the conversation of political ethics from a preoccupation with techniques, programs, and processes to manage nation-state politics in Africa. Transitional justice mechanisms operate on this level of prescriptive recommendations to repair the violent legacy of Africa's politics. Angelina Atyam's story points to and operates on what one might call a more elemental level of political engagement, which has to do with the underlying visions and stories that drive Africa's political modernity. In the end what Atyam's story reveals is that to stop the endless cycles of war and violence in Africa requires a radical interruption of politics as we know it by visions of human society emerging, as it were, from a "different planet." Instead of a politics that assumes fighting and the pursuit of power as inevitable, Angelina Atyam's story is an invitation into another kind of politics—politics as participation in the self-sacrificing and reconciling righteousness of God.

---

[24]Interview by the author, *Pilgrimage of Pain and Hope*, July 29, 2009.

[25]For a discussion of these and similar questions, see, e.g., Simon Wiesenthal's moving book *The Sunflower: On the Possibilities and Limits of Forgiveness*, rev. ed. (New York: Schocken, 1998).

3

The End of Words

Reconciliation in the Wake of Genocide in Rwanda

The Deafening Silence

I remember my first visit to Rwanda after the 1994 genocide. It was July 1998. As the small plane started its descent to the Gregoire Kayibanda Airport to end the short flight from Entebbe, I thought of the events of 1994. It must have been around this same time (7:30 p.m.), I recalled, when the plane carrying President Habyarimana was shot down somewhere around here as he returned from peace negotiations in Arusha. It was this event that set in motion the series of events that resulted in the slaughter of over 800,000 Rwandans in less than a hundred days.

I stepped from the plane into the cool air of the evening and followed the line of other passengers as we walked to the terminal building. We walked in silence. Inside the small terminal, the passport control officer checked my passport, stamped it, and handed it back to me without saying anything. I stepped out of the terminal building and immediately recognized the van with the Novatel logo. As I approached the van, the driver welcomed me, took my bag, and opened the door for me to get in. He started the

This essay originated as the keynote address at *The Other Journal's* Faith, Film, Justice Forum in Seattle, October 16–18, 2009. Reprinted with permission from *The Other Journal,* http://theotherjournal.com.

van, and as we pulled out, he asked me where I was from. I told him I was from Uganda. He wanted to know how things were in Uganda. I in turn asked him how things were in Rwanda. He told me things were better. I tried to strike a conversation beyond this initial exchange but could not get very far. He apologized because his English was not good. I apologized because I did not know Kinyarwanda. As we drove in silence, I blamed myself for not having learned enough Kinyarwanda from my parents, who were originally from Rwanda. I also blamed myself for not having learned enough French during the six years I studied in Belgium. We drove on in silence to the hotel.

Over the next three days, as I visited different historical places and genocide sites in Rwanda, I was glad to have Joseph, my guide and translator, with me, to show me different places, explain the history of Rwanda, and introduce me to the social, historical, and cultural complexities of Rwanda. Even as I had Joseph with me and was thus able to "talk" and interact with many people, there was still a silence in and about Rwanda that was striking. The silence took many forms. First, everywhere we went people were generally quiet and reserved. There was not the usual boisterous interaction that one often finds in African villages and towns. Even the visible presence and proximity to one another seemed characterized by a sense of distance and aloofness. Second, even as people shared their stories of survival (or memory of "those days"), there was always a point at which people just fell silent (often in the middle of a story). Moreover, even as I visited places, and talked to different people, I had a feeling of being watched, examined, interrogated, but in silence. It was as if the entire land was enveloped in this mysterious silence that affected, infected, and defined everything—every interaction and every communication. At times, the silence was almost deafening.

That was 1998, and I had gone to Rwanda as a scholar and researcher. I have since returned to Rwanda on numerous occasions, but not as a researcher/scholar, but as a pilgrim (since 2004 I have been organizing and leading "pilgrimages of pain and hope" to Rwanda).[1] And whereas the silence in Rwanda has continued

---

[1] For more on the pilgrimages of pain and hope, see my "Mission and the Ephesian Moment of World Christianity: Pilgrimages of Pain and Hope and the Economics of Eating Together," *Mission Studies* 29, no. 2 (2012): 183–200.

to strike me as particularly acute, in the context of the pilgrimage journeys, the silence has taken on a deeper significance. I have come to see that the silence of Rwanda is not so much the effect of a failure to communicate because of linguistic limitations; nor is it a silence of one trying to guard or hold onto a delicate secret. It is the silence of lament, and thus one that is filled with theological significance. Accordingly, whereas before as a scholar, I had been scared by the silence, as a pilgrim, I now approach the silence with sacred awe. For like Moses before the burning bush, I feel myself both invited and yet cautioned about stepping too callously into the holy presence of the burning bush of silence. Where before as a scholar, I had been intent on blasting through Rwanda and Rwanda's history, looking for explanations, searching for answers and for lessons and solutions, I now see that the invitation is to take off my sandals, sit down, so to say, to slow down my quest for explanations, and the preoccupation with programs and models of successful mission and reconstruction.

As a pilgrim, as I have been invited to sit in the silence, I have found myself wondering with the psalmist about an uncertain future: "When the foundations are destroyed, what can the just do?" (Ps 11:3). The silence was what was allowing me to see the depth of the pain in Rwanda. Whereas before I looked on Rwanda from the outside and saw Rwanda as but a case of tragic history, I began to identify with the pain as my own. As I did, I was moved to tears and learned to cry with and on behalf of Rwanda. The words of Jeremiah, the wailing prophet, in relation to Jerusalem had become my own words in relation to Rwanda: "Let my eyes run down with tears night and day, and let them not cease. For the virgin daughter of my people is shattered with a great wound, with a very grievous blow" (Jer 14:17).

The Resounding Success of Rwanda

The more I became a pilgrim into Rwanda's pain, the more I became bothered, on my subsequent visits to Rwanda, with the noise that tried to cover it up. If in 1998 it was the silence of Rwanda that bothered me, in a 2009 visit it was the noise of, from, and about Rwanda that bothered me. Everywhere I turned, so it seemed, there was a story, an article, an essay, a film, or a book that described the amazing transformation of Rwanda, with a description of programs, initiatives, and the impressive stories of forgiveness and reconciliation that are helping make Rwanda a success story.[2] Airports were filled with investors making their way to Rwanda to set up micro credit, finance, and telecommunications businesses. All mission roads led to Rwanda, so it seemed, as Western churches sent mission teams in droves to Rwanda: Rick Warren and his Saddleback-based PEACE program attracted a lot of attention. New ultramodern shopping malls opened in Kigali offering twenty-four-hour shopping, ATMs, Western-style bookstores, and coffee shops. New gated and high-end neighborhoods, like Nyaraturama on the outskirts of Kigali, sprang up. Paul Kagame's vision to make Rwanda the IT hub of the East African region seems to be working, with Kagame offering a model of disciplined leadership, zero tolerance for corruption, and a mixture of social engineering and innovative social entrepreneurship. The combined effect of all these developments seems to confirm that years after the genocide, a new future in Rwanda is already here. The silence of genocide has been transformed into a resounding cacophony of success.

The image of the new Rwanda and the sense of resounding success was brought home to me in July 2010 in Kigali as I attended the concert to mark the end of the nationally instituted one hundred days of mourning, which was held in Amahoro stadium. The stadium was packed with mostly youthful Rwandans, swaying with hands in the air and singing along with Andrew Palau's band blasting loud Christian music. The concert was at once an expression and a metaphor of the healing and success of Rwanda.

We love such celebrations and other stories of success out of Rwanda for they relieve us of the need to engage the silence of genocide. By this silence I do not only mean the silence of Western betrayal during the 1994 genocide, but also the silence of postgenocide Rwanda, which keeps inviting us into its painful but mysterious grace of lament. Entering this space of silence and lament requires us to learn to be pilgrims and not be either

---

[2]On such stories, see, for example, Catherine Claire Larson, *As We Forgive: Stories of Reconciliation from Rwanda* (Grand Rapids, MI: Zondervan, 2009); John Rucyahana, *The Bishop of Rwanda* (Nashville, TN: Thomas Nelson, 2007).

bystanders or agents of salvation. We are afraid to be pilgrims, because we do not know how to enter the silence of our own pain, betrayal, or destruction. We keep hoping that there might be a program, a set of skills and mechanisms—justice, reconciliation, forgiveness—that might transport us into a new future of restoration without the need to sit in and within the silence of lament. And the more we look for such mechanisms, the more we skirt around the need and role of the church. That is why the fascination with the language of "reconciliation," "forgiveness," and "justice" in Rwanda ironically both obscures and marginalizes the necessary theological and ecclesiological nature of the church—as a community born within the silence of lament. But without such communities and the rich range of practices that constitutes their liturgical life we face the constant danger of "dealing lightly with the wounds" of God's people—announcing peace, a new future, where no such future exists (Jer 6:14).

Discerning the Silence

In the midst of the success of Rwanda, the silence is still there, only now more difficult to see, hear, or discern. During a visit to Rwanda in the summer of 2010, as we drove from Kigali to Goma, Juliet (name changed to protect her true identity), our Rwandan partner with the Great Lakes Initiative, explained to us the hopes of Kagame's vision to transform Rwanda into a modern and self-sufficient economy. At one time in the conversation I asked Juliet how the people, especially in the rural areas, were responding to Kagame's vision, particularly the optimism reflected in the saying "Rwandans do not have to walk, they can run."

Many are simply overwhelmed, Juliet confirmed. "It is a lot of changes much too fast." However, she went on, "This is not our major problem. The greatest problem of this country," she said, "is silence. Many feel that their story has no place in Rwanda. They follow the government policies, they gather at rallies and sing the government slogans, but they are keeping a distance from everything."

Since I found Juliet's remarks quite telling, I engaged her further around the issue of silence and why she thought this was a major problem in Rwanda.

"Genocide destroyed us," Juliet said. "You see the people who killed during the genocide. . . . Many killed not out of hatred. They loved their neighbors whom they killed. Many killed because of fear. Many were led to believe that their own lives were in danger. The heightened propaganda succeeded in bringing many people to a state of hysterical fear: 'kill or be killed.' As a result, generally peaceful people killed their neighbors. Christians killed Christians; others killed members of their own families. It is as if a beast that no one suspected lurked within these ordinarily peaceful people was all of sudden let loose."

And then she continued, "The genocide has thrown all of us now, even those of us who never participated in the genocide, into an identity crisis." I asked her what she meant by that. "I do not mean the identity crisis of whether I am Hutu or Tutsi," she explained. "All of us in Rwanda are Hutsi—both Hutu and Tutsi: there have been (always) intermarriages, and at any rate, it is the clan more than the notions of Hutu and Tutsi that were the basis of social identification in Rwanda. People felt more loyalty to clan than the fact of being Hutu and Tutsi. Clans in Rwanda had both Hutu and Tutsi."

The identity crisis that Juliet was talking about had to do with a sense of uncertainty about one's identity. She explained: "We had always thought of ourselves as good, decent, and peace-loving individuals," she said. "Now I keep asking myself: 'Who am I?' 'Can I trust myself to be a decent, good human being? Or is there a beast within me that will one day take over and lead me into the sort of madness that we witnessed during the genocide? I find that I cannot fully trust myself, even less my neighbor. I must now live with this permanent cloud of uncertainty."

"The genocide destroyed that sense of trust in us," she concluded. And then she added after a while, "It also destroyed something about the sacredness of life."

After a long silence in which both Juliet and I reflected on her words, she told the story of a young girl who survived the genocide, but witnessed many people being killed. After the genocide she told her mother who also had survived the genocide, "Mama, I thought that human beings were different. But they are like banana trees. For I saw that when people were cut down, they fell down just like banana trees. They are not different!"

I reconstruct this conversation with Juliet because it helps confirm the silence that is an inevitable mark of postgenocide Rwanda, but also how this silence is not an "empty" silence—but a silence that bubbles with a lot of unanswered questions about the meaning, dignity, and sacredness of the human person. Who am I? What does it mean to be a human being? Are we indeed different from banana trees? Is it true that we are created in the image of God? What does that mean? Is that true for the killers as well? Who is my neighbor, and what does it mean to be a neighbor? Whom can I trust?

These questions relate to the very foundation of what it means to be human. Many of us take these questions for granted, but they are the basis on which our social interactions, our religious beliefs and expressions, and our ethical convictions and principles are built, and these foundations have been shaken, even destroyed by the genocide experience. This is what makes it impossible to talk meaningfully about such notions as peace, reconciliation, justice, and truth in the wake of genocide. In other words, in the wake of genocide we cannot expect notions like "forgiveness," "justice," and "reconciliation" to bear the burden of carrying us from the silence that genocide brings to the sunny promises of a new future which we desperately long for. To put the argument even more pointedly, there can be no forgiveness, no justice, no reconciliation in the wake of genocide, because the very foundations on which these notions are built are destroyed by the experience of genocide.[3]

Lament and Restoration:
The Church in the Valley of Dry Bones

To put the argument more constructively: Genocide brings us to the end of words, and the only language at the end of words is the language of lament. It is the church's unique calling and gift to live into and invite others into this space of silence and lament in a way that can be hopeful, which is to say, a way that leads neither to self-destructive nihilism or total isolation, but to a hope for healing and restoration. In order to be able to do so,

---

[3]This is the issue that Simon Wiesenthal wrestles with in *The Sunflower: On the Possibilities and Limits of Forgiveness*, rev. exp. ed. (New York: Schocken Books, 1998).

the church must learn from the prophet Ezekiel about what it means to stand in the valley of dry bones (Ez 37).

The hand of the LORD was upon me, and he brought me out by the Spirit of the LORD and set me in the middle of a valley; it was full of bones. He led me back and forth among them, and I saw a great many bones on the floor of the valley, bones that were very dry. He asked me, "Son of man, can these bones live?" I said, "O Sovereign LORD, you alone know."

Then he said to me, "Prophesy to these bones and say to them, 'Dry bones, hear the word of the LORD! This is what the Sovereign LORD says to these bones: I will make breath enter you, and you will come to life. I will attach tendons to you and make flesh come upon you and cover you with skin; I will put breath in you, and you will come to life. Then you will know that I am the LORD.'"

So I prophesied as I was commanded. And as I was prophesying, there was a noise, a rattling sound, and the bones came together, bone to bone. I looked, and tendons and flesh appeared on them and skin covered them, but there was no breath in them.

Then he said to me, "Prophesy to the breath; prophesy, son of man, and say to it, 'This is what the Sovereign LORD says: Come from the four winds, O breath, and breathe into these slain, that they may live.'" So I prophesied as he commanded me, and breath entered them; they came to life and stood up on their feet—a vast army.

Then he said to me: "Son of man, these bones are the whole house of Israel. They say, 'Our bones are dried up and our hope is gone; we are cut off.' Therefore prophesy and say to them: 'This is what the Sovereign LORD says: O my people, I am going to open your graves and bring you up from them; I will bring you back to the land of Israel. Then you, my people, will know that I am the LORD, when I open your graves and bring you up from them. I will put my Spirit in you and you will live, and I will settle you in your own land. Then you will know that I the LORD have spoken, and I have done it, declares the LORD.'"

A priest (in Jerusalem) turned prophet, Ezekiel was carried into exile in 597 BC. It is from exile that he delivers the prophecy to his fellow Israelites in exile. There are a number of elements about the prophecy that evoke the situation of postgenocide Rwanda. Accordingly, there are a number of aspects of Ezekiel's life in general and his standing and actions in the valley of dry bones in particular that point to the church's calling and confirm why the church is best suited to engage the silence of Rwanda, and how the church might best do that. First, more than any biblical prophet, Ezekiel was given to symbolic actions, strange visions, and trances. He eats the scroll on which words of prophecy are written (3:1–3); he lies down for extended periods (4:4ff.) He took the potter's flask and smashed it (to symbolize Israel's being scattered). That Ezekiel was given to symbolic actions, visions, and trances indicates the "language" of the church in postgenocide time: a language of symbols, parables, and sacraments.

Second, Ezekiel's prophecy is born out of silence. Earlier in his ministry, Ezekiel was struck dumb for an unspecified period of time (3:26). It is the same Ezekiel who was struck dumb who is now brought to the valley of dry bones. This is, of course, the valley of death, of silence. He must first learn to stand in silence before he is ordered to prophesy. The church of Ezekiel is a church that is both invited into silence, and yet ordered to prophesy. That Ezekiel was able to live in this call of silence and prophecy might be partly due to his double identity as priest and prophet. In this double role, the prophet serves as the embodiment of the history, suffering, despair, and hope of his people. This partly explains a number of the symbolic actions of the prophet. He is carried into exile; he lies down (symbolizing the death of his people). His wife dies in exile. The valley of dry bones in which Ezekiel is forced to stand is the valley of his own and his people's death.

Third, when Ezekiel is asked whether the bones could live, his honest answer was "I am not sure, for they look pretty dead to me." Involved in Ezekiel's response is the awareness that he himself has come to the limits of his own calling. In his repertoire of prophetic/priestly/ministry tools, he has no trick, no magic wand, no word, no formula that could bring about the restoration. That is when, at the end of his ministry, he is asked—nay commanded to prophesy.

Fourth, the nature of Ezekiel's prophecy is significant. He is commanded to "summon the wind from the four corners." Just as the act of creation in Genesis begins with the wind—the "ruah" hovering over the formless void (Gen 1:1), and with God's breath into Adam (Gen 2),these images in Ezekiel evoke the promise and possibility of new creation (re-creation) even in the valley of dry bones. Ezekiel's role in the drama is to summon (invite) the spirit of God's creation. And as Ezekiel did so, there was a noise, a rattling sound, as the bones began to come together. The restoration comes as a gift from God: "When I open your graves and make you come from them, then you will know that I am the Lord."

All these elements point to the critical role of the church, more specifically to the practice of worship as the space and place through which the silence arising from the experience of genocide might be engaged in a way that calls forth (summons) God's re-creating spirit within its dry bones. For it is in worship that the church not only receives the story of Ezekiel, but also lives into its reality. In worship the church is brought to silence as it is invited (nay forced) to look into and admit its own brokenness and the brokenness of the world—and thus seek God's mercy and healing. But in worship the church is also invited to shout aloud and sing God's praises. So in worship Christians are able to at once sit in silence and shout out aloud, to sit alone and yet together with others in the valley of death. In worship Christians relive the past in a way that is already taken up in God's future as they proclaim both that Christ has died and is risen. What this means is that in worship both lament and trust, pain and hope, the crucifixion and the resurrection come together in a way that breathes new life in our own valley of dry bones. And yet this is not to say that worship is the trick, the formula that carries us from the valley to the sunny promise of resurrection. For this happens as a gift.

For as we come before and in the presence of Christ who is both priest and prophet, as we sing together psalms of our desperation and shattered hopes, as we celebrate the supper of the lamb who was slain but now is risen and invites us to receive him at his banquet, we discover that *somehow* we have been re-membered, reconstituted, and even reconciled to one another. That as we participate in these practices and movements called worship, we discover *somehow* that our identity as children of God has been reaffirmed as we behold God's own son on the cross. As we grasp this gift, we discover that we have *somehow* already received the grace of forgiveness.

I say *somehow* because forgiveness is not so much a card that victims hold and which they can pass out at the appropriate time to deserving perpetrators; it is more of a gift that we receive and invite others into. But I also say *somehow*, because that gift is never complete; it is never total. It is an ongoing journey. And so, through worship, one learns to speak about the gift in terms of "signs." But that forgiveness is never complete does not make the signs any less real. Worship trains us to recognize these signs also as "sacraments"—real, visible, concrete expressions of something deeper. That is why the space of worship is also the space of "parables" (it is like a mustard seed or leaven). If worship invites us into the space and place of lament, it invites us into a journey of hope. In and through that practice we begin to experience the real. New creation is always experienced as broken, incomplete, and fragmentary, as here but not here, as an eschatological reality.

To be honest, I do not know how the notions of justice, reconciliation, forgiveness, and even truth might appear to the young girl of Juliet's story in the absence of a sacramentally rich worshipping community. For the time of Rwanda, like the time of Ezekiel, is a time that calls for a space and place for lament. Such a space, as the life of Ezekiel shows, is a place for silence and tears, a place for prophecy, which is to say for summoning God's re-creating spirit; a time and space for signs and symbols and for hope and visions of restoration. In the absence of such a space and place for lament and restoration, it seems to be asking too much for a notion (justice, reconciliation) or any program—including the highly-touted traditional justice system (known as Gacaca)—to bear the burden of carrying Rwandans from the valley of death to the promise of a new future. That would be expecting Gacaca to function as a church, which of course it is not.

4

Reconciling *Africae Munus*

The Church in Africa in Service to Reconciliation, Justice, and Peace

An Apostolic Exhortation

On November 19, 2011, Pope Benedict XVI published the Post-Synodal Apostolic Exhortation *Africae Munus*, marking the climax of the Second Synod of Bishops on Africa.[1] The synod was held in Rome (October 4–25, 2009). The title was "The Church in Africa in Service to Reconciliation, Justice, and Peace."[2] The exhortation has two parts. Part 1 (14–96)[3] identifies the mission of the church, which has its origin in the person of Jesus Christ, who, through his passion, death, and resurrection, reconciled

---

This essay is reprinted with permission from *Mission as Ministry of Reconciliation*, ed. Robert Schreiter and Knud Jorgensen (London: Regnum Books International, 2013), 66–78.

[1] The exhortation builds on the theme of the First Synod of Bishops for Africa (held in Rome in 1994), which focused on the "Church as Family of God." See John Paul II, Post-Synodal Apostolic Exhortation, *Ecclesia in Africa*, http://www.vatican.va.

[2] Attended by over 135 participants, including two cardinals, forty-two bishops, priests, and laypeople from forty-six countries of Africa, the full title of the Synod was "The Church in Africa at the Service of Reconciliation, Justice, and Peace: 'You are the salt of the earth . . . You are the light of the world' (Mt 5:13, 14)."

[3] All parenthetical references to *Africae Munus* refer to numbered paragraphs within the original document. The exhortation is available at the Vatican website: http://www.vatican.va.

man with God and with neighbor. Listening to him, Christians are invited to be reconciled with God, becoming just in order to build a peaceable society and committing themselves to fraternal service for love of truth, which is the source of peace. Part 2 (97–177) addresses different sections of the church in Africa (bishops, priests, deacons, laypeople, etc.), identifying priority areas of ministry and inviting each to promote reconciliation, justice, and peace in the church and in society.

The simple structure might easily hide the fact that *Africae Munus* is a complex document, which not only underlines the need for reconciliation, justice, and peace in Africa but also reinforces the ecclesial dynamism of Africa, while outlining a program for pastoral activity for the coming decades of evangelization. It addresses everyone and everything about the church's mission in Africa. But this is also what makes this compact document a challenging one in terms of a simple and coherent vision of reconciliation as a paradigm for mission in Africa in the twenty-first century. First, although the need for reconciliation, justice, and peace is the clear focus of the first part of document, the second part is dedicated to more general pastoral guidelines, and often with very little explicit reference or connection to the first part. Second, although *Africae Munus* issues an explicit appeal for the church and Christians to pursue reconciliation, justice, and peace, the kind of gift it is for Africa is not made completely explicit. On the contrary, the preoccupation of *Africae Munus* with the church's "mission" and with "pastoral guidelines" easily leads to an impression of reconciliation as simply a pastoral agenda (among many), albeit an urgent and timely one. In this way, *Africae Munus* reflects the tone of the Final Message of the synod, which encouraged each bishop "to put issues of reconciliation, justice and peace high up on the pastoral agenda of his diocese."[4] But reconciliation should not be viewed only as a priority area of the church's mission: it is the lens through which the church (in Africa and elsewhere) understands its identity and mission in the world.

It is important to keep in mind that *Africae Munus* is a *post-synodal apostolic exhortation*. As such, it is a document that is the climax of a long process, the conclusion of a long "ecclesial

---

[4]Message to the People of God of the Second Special Assembly for Africa of the Synod of Bishops, 19. Available at http://www.vatican.va.

conversation,"[5] and thus it assumes and makes references to statements contained in various documents generated before, during, and after the synod.[6] Additionally, the context, genre, style, and purpose of an exhortation preclude any systematic and extensive treatment of its theme. As an apostolic exhortation, *Africae Munus* is a reflection, an extended sermon, in which the pope speaks as a pastor and offers guidelines, recommendations, directives, and exhortations to the church, drawing on theological, pastoral, and liturgical insights informed by scripture and by the church's tradition. Without a sense of the context, process, and rich sources that inform *Africae Munus*, the reader is bound to find it a frustrating document on many levels.

In this essay, while filling out some of this background, I wish to make explicit why reconciliation is a unique gift and vision of hope for the world and Africa in particular. I shall do this by outlining six theses around which a vision and practice of reconciliation is pursued. My aim is not only to offer a framework within which the various recommendations and exhortations of *Africae Munus* make sense, but to suggest this as the kind of framework that is needed if we are to recover reconciliation as a fresh gift and a paradigm for mission in our time.

Thesis One: Reconciliation Is a Gift

Africa's memory and experience of various traumas and conflicts make reconciliation a particularly urgent and timely gift. In part 1 of *Africae Munus* Pope Benedict speaks of Africa as ex-

---

[5]Agbonkhianmeghe E. Orobator, "The Synod as an Ecclesial Conversation," introduction to *Reconciliation, Justice, and Peace: The Second African Synod*, ed. A. E. Orobator (Maryknoll, NY: Orbis Books, 2011).

[6]The preparation for the 2009 synod began in 2005 with an announcement. Following the announcement, a document of Guidelines for Discussion, or *Lineamenta*, was distributed in advance of the synod "to foster extensive discussion on the synodal topic." A working document was prepared from the responses to the questionnaire included in the *Lineamenta*. It is this working document, the *Instrumentum Laboris*, that guided the discussion at the synod. At the end of the synod, the bishops and other participants prepared "Propositions" that were submitted to the pope to help him prepare the post-synodal exhortation. The synod itself generated a number of critical documents; among others is the *Nuntius* or Message of the Synod—the official post-synodal message of the bishops of Africa to the people of Africa. The documents are available on the Vatican website. Another good source is http://www.maryknollafrica.org.

periencing an "anthropological crisis" (11). This crisis, arising to some extent out of Africa's painful memory of fratricidal conflicts between ethnic groups, the slave trade, and colonization (9) is also connected to current problems such as alcohol and drug abuse, malaria, HIV/AIDS, environment pollution, political corruption, unjust economic structures, and globalization—all of which pose a serious threat to life in Africa. Using a biblical image (147–49), Pope Benedict compares Africa to the paralytic in Mark's Gospel (2:1–12), and like the four men who brought the paralytic to Jesus, the church is called to mobilize spiritual energies and material resources to relieve Africa's heavy burden and open Africans to the fullness of life in Christ.[7] The recommendations in part 2 of *Africae Munus*—addressed to the various constituents of the church (99–146)—must be read within the context of crisis and as an invitation to the church to stand in solidarity and creativity in order to remove the obstacles to Africa's healing.

The depiction of Africa's anthropological crisis in *Africae Munus* is powerful. Even more powerful is the conclusion that behind and connected to various social and human challenges lies a *spiritual crisis* of identity. Echoing Peter in the Acts of the Apostles, Pope Benedict notes:

> What Africa needs most is neither gold nor silver; she wants to stand up, like the man at the pool of Bethzatha; she wants to have confidence in herself and in her dignity as a people loved by her God. It is this encounter with Jesus which the church must offer to bruised and wounded hearts yearning for reconciliation and peace, and thirsting for justice. We must prove and proclaim the word of Christ which heals, sets free and reconciles. (149)

It is the need for a new identity (a new vision of itself—as God's beloved) and a new confidence in itself and its dignity that makes reconciliation a unique and rare gift for Africa. For reconciliation is not simply a program or set of skills; it is first and foremost an invitation to experience the new world that God has made

---

[7]In *Ecclesia in Africa*, no. 41, John Paul compared Africa to the man who fell among brigands and called on church and society to be a good Samaritan to Africa.

possible. It is this new world—the New Creation—that Paul talks about in 2 Corinthians 5:16–20:

> So from now on we regard no one from a worldly point of view. Though we once regarded Christ in this way, we do so no longer. Therefore, if anyone is in Christ, the new creation has come: The old has gone, the new is here! All this is from God, who reconciled us to himself through Christ and gave us the ministry of reconciliation: that God was reconciling the world to himself in Christ, not counting people's sins against them. And he has committed to us the message of reconciliation. We are therefore Christ's ambassadors, as though God were making his appeal through us. We implore you on Christ's behalf: Be reconciled to God. (NIV)

The key reality that Paul is announcing here is not, in fact, reconciliation, but the "New Creation." Reconciliation[8] is the way through which God has made this new creation possible, and it is the gift that makes it possible for "anyone in Christ" to belong to this new creation of restored relationships. Reconciliation therefore does not relate, in the first place, to mission (what we should *do*), but to *gift* ("All this is from God") and to invitation—to a new experience of God, of ourselves with one another, and with the whole of creation. Only later in the passage does Paul speak about mission in terms of the service (*diakonia*) of reconciliation being "entrusted to us" as though we were God's ambassadors.

Although *Africae Munus* makes reference to sections from 2 Corinthians (particularly 5:19–20), the notion of "new creation" as the end (the telos) of God's reconciling work is not explicitly invoked, and so the fact that reconciliation is a gift is not emphasized enough. Nevertheless, it is the experience of reconciliation as a gift made possible in Christ that Pope Benedict points to as the ground of Africa's true identity, the source of its dignity, and the basis of its mission in the world. Referring to Africa as a

---

[8] According to Richard B. Hays, "When Paul uses the verb 'reconcile' with God as its subject, he is declaring that God has launched a dramatic new diplomatic initiative to overcome human alienation and to establish new and peaceful relationships." "Reconciliation: The Heart of the Gospel," *Divinity* (Spring 2012): 3. Available at http://divinity.duke.edu.

"spiritual lung" for humanity Benedict notes that if Africa "is to stand erect with dignity, [it] needs to hear the voice of Christ who today proclaims love of neighbour, love of even one's enemies, to the point of laying down one's life" (13).

If reconciliation is then a gift and invitation into a new identity, and thus a fresh starting point for Africa, the primary question that relates to mission as reconciliation is how can Africa receive, enter into, and operate within this experience of new creation so as to live true to its identity and calling? In the remaining part of this essay, drawing from the exhortations of *Africae Munus*, I suggest five other theses that explore the practices and disciplines that sustain reconciliation as a way of life.

Thesis Two: Reconciliation Requires Living into God's Story

The telos within which reconciliation operates as a gift and invitation is, then, the *shalom* of God's new creation. Belonging to this new creation involves a way of seeing and being in the world. Reconciliation is thus not simply a program, but a way of life. As a way of life, reconciliation is lived around scripture and the life of the sacraments, realities that bring Christians in contact with, and ground them deeply into, the story of new creation, which, as Paul notes, is realized "in Christ." It is this basic conviction that the synod delegates are pointing to when they state:

> Reconciliation involves a way of life (spirituality) and a mission. To implement a spirituality of reconciliation, justice and peace, the Church needs witnesses deeply rooted in Christ, nourished by his Word and by the sacraments.[9]

The same conviction is reflected in the numerous scriptural references in *Africae Munus* as well as the specific recommendation for a "biblical apostolate [to] be promoted in each Christian community, in the family and in the ecclesiastical movements" (150), and that "each member of Christ's faithful should grow accustomed to reading the Bible daily" (151). To the youth, the

---

[9]Proposition 9 from the 2009 Second African Synod. Available at http://cpn. nd.edu.

pope offers a similar exhortation: "we need to help young people to gain confidence and familiarity with the sacred Scripture so it can become a compass pointing out the path to follow" (61).

If there is no reconciliation without scripture, there can also be no reconciliation without a life of the sacraments, particularly the Eucharist. Word and Eucharist, Benedict explains,

> are so deeply bound together that we cannot understand one without the other: the word of God takes flesh sacramentally in the event of the Eucharist. The Eucharist opens us to an understanding of Scripture, just as Scripture for its part illumines and explains the mystery of the Eucharist. (40)

The centrality of Word and Eucharist in *Africae Munus* confirms reconciliation as a thick theological praxis, which when abstracted from its scriptural and liturgical matrix loses its force and easily generates into a mere program, a mediation skill (which one picks up and puts down as needed), or simply a convenient political mechanism. But as *Africae Munus* makes clear: "Reconciliation is a pre-political concept and a pre-political reality" (19). This of course does not mean that it has no political import. On the contrary, "for this very reason it is of the greatest importance to the task of politics itself" (19). In other words, the world of God's new creation does not simply conform to current political realities, but it has the power to *reshape* these political realities. That is why, in relation to the challenge of tribalism in Africa, *Africae Munus* calls not simply for "peaceful co-existence" between tribes, but for a new vision of community beyond tribal identity. Thus, Benedict writes:

> Beyond differences of origin or culture, the great challenge facing us all is to discern in the human person, loved by God, the basis of a communion that respects and integrates the particular contributions of different cultures. We "*must really open these boundaries between tribes, ethnic groups and religions to the universality of God's love.*" Men and women, in the variety of their origins, cultures, languages and religions, are capable of living together in harmony. (39, emphasis mine)

It is this possibility of a new sociality, beyond tribalism, that the Holy Trinity Peace Village in Kuron confirms. Founded by retired Bishop Paride Taban in a remote part of Southern Sudan, Holy Trinity Village brings together people from different tribes and religions—Muslims, Christians, Traditionalists—in a cooperative village, where they live, raise their children, and work together with a school, a health clinic, clean water, agricultural projects, and so on. Paride calls the village a "small oasis of peace" (in a country torn by ethnic and religious violence) and an example of the harmony and peace that is reflected in the communion and peaceful relations of the three persons of the Trinity (thus the name "Holy Trinity" Peace Village).[10]

What Taban is doing is to stand within the story of God's reconciling love as revealed in the Trinity and improvise out of that story concrete initiatives that that not only affirm the inherent dignity of Africans, but open up fresh possibilities of peace and flourishing in the context of tribalism, war, and poverty.

Thesis Three: Reconciliation Is Advocacy Grounded in Lament and Conversion

Even though the gift of new creation is real, Africans continue to live in a world marked by divisions, racism, tribalism, hatred, and violence. Reconciliation is therefore grounded in lament, which involves the ability see honestly, name truthfully, and to stand within the broken world of our day-to-day existence, and yet not despair in the reality of new creation. It is within this spirit of lament that the synod delegates offered a somber assessment of Africa:

> While "rich in human and natural resources, many of our people are still left to wallow in poverty and misery, wars and conflicts, crises and chaos." These evils, the Synod asserts, are mainly the product of "human decisions and activities by people who have no regard for the common good and this often through a tragic complicity and criminal conspiracy of local leaders and foreign interests."[11]

---

[10]See my *The Sacrifice of Africa: A Political Theology for Africa* (Grand Rapids, MI: Eerdmans, 2010), 135–47.

[11]Michael McCabe, SMA, "The Second African Synod: Major Emphases and

Even without using the language of lament, in its extensive depiction of Africa's anthropological crisis *Africae Munus* was able to ground the search for reconciliation in the painful reality of Africa's present situation. What is perhaps even more significant is the acknowledgment that Christians are implicated in the crisis. As one of the delegates, Archbishop Palmer-Buckle of Ghana, stated: "The church has transformed neither society nor itself. . . . Where there has been corruption, Catholics have been involved, and where there has been violence Catholics have been among those instigating it."[12] *Africae Munus* captured the sentiment more mildly by noting that Christians are affected by the spirit and customs of their time and place (32).

The acknowledgment of the church's limitations and failures is not a cause for despair. It is an opportunity for conversion, which, as *Africae Munus* notes, "is a necessary condition for the transformation of the world" (103). But conversion is not merely turning away from evil and sinfulness; authentic conversion or *metanoia* is turning toward God the Father, "the source of true life, who alone is capable of delivering us from evil and all temptations, and keeping us in his Spirit, in the very heart of the struggle against the forces of evil" (32). That is why a call to conversion is not a form of escapism into the spiritual realm. For the more grounded one is in the story of God, the more clearly one is able to assess the limits and contradictions of the current social systems, and the more strengthened one becomes in one's commitment to build a more just society.

Throughout *Africae Munus* there is a tension that the pope tries to navigate. On the one hand, Pope Benedict encourages Christians to take their faith seriously as the foundation for building a more just and peaceful African society. But on the other, he notes that the church "does not have technical solutions to offer and does not claim to 'interfere in any way in the politics of states'" (22). The pursuit of a just and peaceful society walks the tightrope between the reality of a world reconciled and the hard realities of politics and economics historically construed. In his closing remarks at the end of the synod, Benedict noted:

Challenges," message no. 5. Available at http://www.missiologia.org.
    [12]Ibid.

The theme "Reconciliation, justice, and peace" certainly implies a strong political dimension, even if it is obvious that reconciliation, justice and peace are not possible without a deep purification of the heart, without renewal of thought, a "metanoia," without something new that can only come from the encounter with God. But even if this spiritual dimension is profound and fundamental, the political dimension is also very real, because without political achievements, these changes of the Spirit usually are not realized. Therefore the temptation could have been in politicizing the theme, to talk less about pastors and more about politicians, thus with a competence that is not ours. The other danger was—to avoid this temptation—pulling oneself into a purely spiritual world, in an abstract and beautiful world, but not a realistic one.[13]

What one senses behind Benedict's remarks is not simply an attempt to hedge church-state relations, but rather a recognition of the inevitable "in-between" within which a vision of reconciliation is lived: between the already and the not yet; between new creation and the stubborn realities of old creation; between the church's own call and mission to be a sign and sacrament of a world reconciled and the church's own often disappointing witness; between the now and the final realization of a "new heaven and new earth" (Rev 21:3). The observation means that reconciliation will never totally fit; it will constantly be resisted; its vision will seem naïve; its efforts will remain fragile and never completely fulfilled. It is this realization that shapes reconciliation as a form of ongoing advocacy grounded in lament; working within the limits of the present, but always pressing the limits of current political and ecclesial systems toward an expanding social horizon of God's new creation. Elsewhere in *Africae Munus* Benedict speaks about a "revolution" and notes that "Christ does not propose a revolution of a social or political kind, but a revolution of love, brought about by his complete self-giving through his death on the Cross and his resurrection" (26). Reconciliation

---

[13]"Synod for Africa, Penultimate Act: The Final Propositions," October 26, 2009. Available at http://chiesa.espresso.repubblica.it. See also *Africae Munus*, 17.

ferments a revolution of love within the sluggish in-between—a revolution grounded in and carried forth through lament and a life of ongoing conversion.

Thesis Four: Reconciliation Is Work: Sowing and Nurturing Seeds of Hope

Reconciliation is a gift. But it is also work. God has entrusted to us the service of reconciliation: We are therefore Christ's ambassadors. The work of being ambassadors of reconciliation is grounded in the firm conviction that even in the midst of violence, war, and pain, God is always sowing seeds of peace (Is 43:19). The work of peace therefore involves in the first place, learning to see and live in the world with hope. Even as *Africae Munus* names the various social challenges facing Africa, which can seem so daunting, its tonality is one of hope. It invites the church to look at Africa with faith and hope and celebrates God's many gifts to Africa: its spiritual dynamism, its "extraordinary human and spiritual riches . . . [and its] abundant resources" (13).

That noted, the driving assumption behind *Africae Munus* is that to build a reconciled, just, and peaceful African society requires concerted efforts in a variety of areas.[14] Thus, *Africae Munus* lifts up not only the areas where the church has historically played a considerable role in building a peaceful society in Africa (education, health care, communications, etc.) and calls for a doubling of efforts there, it also points to areas of high priority: respect for creation and the ecosystem (79), good governance, empowerment of women (the backbone of Africa's society) (58), positive treatment of children (67), and so on. Additionally, *Africae Munus* offers numerous specific recommendations regarding issues from dialogue with other religions, especially Islam and African Tradition Religions, to the treatment of immigrants and refugees; from recommendations to establish commissions for justice and peace at diocesan and parish levels to the setting up of monitoring desks for prevention and resolution of conflict to

---

[14]There is a preponderance of words like "pursue," "efforts," "contribution," "build," and "seek" in *Africae Munus*.

instituting national and regional peace-building councils. What the recommendations confirm is that even as the vision of reconciliation and peace that informs *Africae Munus* is thoroughly theological, the pursuit of reconciliation is holistic, practical, concrete, and mundane.

However, that the pursuit of reconciliation is practical and mundane does not mean that it should operate according to established canons or culturally accepted norms. In a section addressing bishops, *Africae Munus* warns against the idols of nationalism and of absolutizing African culture. Noting that such idols are an illusion, *Africae Munus* states that they are temptations that can easily lead one to believe that "human efforts alone can bring the Kingdom of eternal happiness on earth" (102). Accordingly, even as it remains practical and concrete, the pursuit of reconciliation, justice, and peace is shaped and sustained by a vision beyond and presses toward a future promised and not yet seen. That is why reconciliation requires, more than experts, witnesses who are

> profoundly rooted in Christ and find nourishment in his word and the sacraments. As they strive to grow in holiness, these witnesses can become engaged in building communion among God's family, communicating to the world—if necessary even to the point of martyrdom—the spirit of reconciliation, justice and peace, after the example of Christ. (34)

A vision and praxis of reconciliation thus requires and involves various efforts (which constitute the search for peace) as well as stories. The stories of witnesses, like the "cloud of witnesses," (Heb 12:1) of scripture teach us the character of hope: the evidence of things not seen (Heb 11:1). But the stories of witnesses also inspire and encourage us in the struggle for a more just and peaceful society, and confirm that the hope of a reconciled, just, and peaceful society, if costly, is nevertheless real! Therefore, part of the work of peace involves naming, celebrating, and preserving the memory of Africa's many witnesses of hope. It is for this reason that *Africae Munus* encourages "pastors of the local Churches to recognize among servants of the Gospel in Africa those who could be canonized" (114).

Thesis Five: Reconciliation, Forgiveness, and Justice Go Hand in Hand

Throughout *Africae Munus* the notions of reconciliation, justice, and peace are held together as the theme of the synod, and the exhortation confirms: "The Church in Africa at the Service of Reconciliation, Justice, and Peace." Although "forgiveness" is not included in the title, both the synod and *Africae Munus* make it clear that there can be no reconciliation (and thus peace) without forgiveness. The reason behind this conclusion is that forgiveness is a natural outcome of God's gift of reconciliation. The delegates thus noted in Proposition 14:

> The fruit of reconciliation between God and humanity, and within the human family itself, is the restoration of justice and the just demands of relationships. This is because God justifies the sinner by overlooking his or her sins, or one justifies an offender by pardoning his or her faults.[15]

This statement not only affirms the interconnectedness of reconciliation and forgiveness, it introduces a fresh logic in the relationship between forgiveness and justice. If we are accustomed to thinking of justice as a prerequisite for forgiveness and reconciliation, here the synod affirmed the priority of forgiveness, noting that just as "God has justified us by forgiving our sins . . . we too can work out just relationships and structures among ourselves and in our societies, through pardoning and overlooking people's faults out of love and mercy. How else can we live in community and communion?"

In *Africae Munus* itself, Benedict reiterates the priority of forgiveness over justice, pointing out that after extended periods of war "it is by granting and receiving forgiveness that the traumatized memories of individuals and communities have found healing and families formerly divided have rediscovered harmony" (21). However, the priority of forgiveness does not mean that the demands of justice must be set aside.

---

[15]Proposition 14, Second African Synod.

If it is to be effective, this reconciliation has to be accompanied by a courageous and honest act: the pursuit of those responsible for these conflicts, those who commissioned crimes and who were involved in trafficking of all kinds, and the determination of their responsibility. Victims have a right to truth and justice. (21)

It is with a similar concern for the demands of justice, that the pope condemns the plunder of Africa's resources as immoral and unjust (24) and calls for more just international relationships, noting that what the world owes Africa is not charity, but more just political and economic structures:

Justice obliges us "to render to each his due." . . . It is an issue, then, of rendering justice to whole peoples. Africa is capable of providing every individual and every nation of the continent with the basic conditions which will enable them to share in development. Africans will thus be able to place their God-given talents and riches at the service of their land and their brothers and sisters. (24)

Even as *Africae Munus* insists that the demands of justice must be met, justice is not an end in itself. Justice must always be inspired and directed by charity—not charity as almsgiving (a charity which fails to respect justice and rights of all is false [18]), but as *caritas*, which is the very essence of God.[16] Caritas, *Africae Munus* notes, not only establishes our bond with God, "it also shows us what true justice is in the act of Christ taking upon himself the faults of sinful humanity so that we may receive in exchange the blessings" that are God's gift (Gal 3:13–14). In a beautiful reflection on the story of Zacchaeus (Lk 19:1–10) Benedict notes that it is this justice of love that must infuse and open up our love of justice to a new horizon. "Divine justice," he notes, "indicates to human justice, limited and imperfect as it is, the horizon to which it must tend if it is to become perfect" (25). Additionally,

---

[16]The theme of *caritas* is at the heart of Pope Benedict's theology. In *Deus Caritas Est,* his very first encyclical as pope, Benedict explores this essence of God, manifested in God's Trinitarian nature, in the work of creation and redemption, and in the church as a community of love.

The social horizon opened up by Christ's work, based on love, surpasses the minimum demands of human justice, that is to say, giving the other his due. The inner logic of love goes beyond this justice, even to the point of giving up one's possessions. (28)

If reconciliation, forgiveness, and justice go hand in hand, a vision of reconciliation must constantly press beyond the "love of justice" toward the" justice of love." The latter is grounded in forgiveness, involves sacrifice, and seeks the salvation of the wrongdoer.

Thesis Six: Reconciliation Requires the Church

The church is not only needed in the pursuit of a just and peaceful society; reconciliation is at the very heart of the life and mission of the church. *Africae Munus* notes various contributions of the church in Africa: its service in the fields of education, health care, and communications; its defense of human rights and dignity; its outreach in offering relief and protection to those need; and its action as sentinel in making "heard the silent cry of the innocent who suffer persecution" (30). However, significant as these various contributions are to the building of a just social order, they are not the primary reason why reconciliation needs the church—otherwise the church would not be different from an NGO. It is precisely with this danger in mind that *Africae Munus* cautions priests against reducing their ministry to one of advocacy or social service: "To yield to the temptation of becoming political leaders or social agents would be to betray your priestly mission and to do a disservice to society, which expects of you prophetic words and deeds" (108).

Since reconciliation is an invitation into the story of God's new creation, the church's primary role is to point to and be a constant reminder of the story of new creation made possible by God's reconciliation. In one of the most moving testimonies of the synod, Sister Uwamariya, reflecting on her experience of meeting and forgiving the person who killed her father during the Rwanda genocide in 1994, captured this unique and essential role of the church:

From this experience I drew the conclusion that reconciliation is not so much bringing together two people or two groups in conflict. Rather it means re-establishing each into love and letting inner healing take place, which then leads to mutual liberation. And here is the importance of the church in our countries since her mission is to give the Word: A Word that heals, sets free, and reconciles.[17]

This unique mission of the church—"to give the Word that heals, sets free, and reconciles"—permeates the text of *Africae Munus*. Even when Benedict notes the church's role as peacemaker, agent of reconciliation, and herald of justice, he adds a reminder that "the Church's mission is not political in nature. Her task is to open the world to the religious sense by proclaiming Christ" (23). Living out that role requires first and foremost that the church becomes the first witness and exemplar of the gift of the Word that heals, sets free, and reconciles. The church is sign and sacrament of that gift. Speaking about peace, the pope notes:

> True peace comes from Christ. It cannot be compared with the peace that the world gives. It is not the fruit of negotiations and diplomatic agreements based on particular interests. It is the peace of a humanity reconciled with itself in God, a peace of which the Church is the sacrament. (30)

The practical import of these observations is to suggest that the church's worship and liturgical practices, its prayer and sacramental life, as well as the scriptural disciplines of meditation on and proclamation of the Word, are essential practices through which the church points to, receives, and celebrates the gift of God's peace. These practices are therefore the primary and nonreplaceable practices through which the church builds peace. They are not the only ones. But unless all other efforts are grounded in, reflect, and are nourished by the church's own experience of a "peace which the world cannot give," those efforts become an endless and futile attempt to be socially relevant,

---

[17] As cited by Paul Bere, "The Word of God as Transformative Power in Reconciling African Christians," in Orobator, *Reconciliation, Justice, and Peace*, 48.

and eventually lose the essential dynamism to sustain them.

It is also this realization of church as sign and sacrament of reconciliation that constantly places the church's own witness under critical scrutiny. This is what *Africae Munus* is pointing to when in calling for ecumenical dialogue it notes that the "path to reconciliation must first pass through the communion of Christ's disciples. A divided Christianity remains a scandal, since it de facto contradicts the will of the Divine Master" (89). This realization also means that the neat laity-clergy divide and the exclusion of women from full participation in the Catholic Church's ministerial and administrative leadership remain issues around which critics will keep pressing for more efforts and actions to promote reconciliation *within* the church.[18]

My goal in this exploration has been to make explicit the conviction that reconciliation is not simply one pastoral program among many, but the lens through which the church understands its identity and mission in the world. The post-synodal exhortation *Africae Munus* reinforces this conviction, and thus provides a timely set of pastoral guidelines and recommendations for the mission of the church in Africa in the twenty-first century. A key assumption behind our discussion has been that a full appreciation of reconciliation as a paradigm for mission requires a framework which not only makes explicit the unique gift that reconciliation is, but also highlights the nonnegotiable elements of that gift. I have pointed to five such elements—story, lament, hope, justice, and forgiveness—important for the church's mission of reconciliation. In exploring these elements, my goal has been to highlight the gifts, practices, and disciplines that sustain a vision and practice of reconciliation. The more immediate objective of my discussion has been to show that within this framework the 2009 synod and the Apostolic Exhortation *Africae Munus* make a historic and highly valuable contribution to the recovery of reconciliation as a unique gift and invitation—a way of seeing and living in the world.

---

[18]See, for example, Teresa Okure, "Church-Family of God: The Place of God's Reconciliation, Justice, and Peace," in Orobator, *Reconciliation, Justice, and Peace*, 13–24: "The church must not only be God's agent proclaiming reconciliation, justice, and peace to the world, but a body that visibly lives, incarnates, and models this divine reconciliation" (15).

PART II

FOR THE LIFE OF THE WORLD

*The Church as Sacrament
of God's Reconciliation
in the World*

5

Parables of a "New We"

Thinking Theologically
about Christian Identity

> Do not conform yourself to this age, but be transformed
> by the renewal of your mind, that you may discern
> what is the will of God, what is good and acceptable
> and perfect.
>
> —Romans 12:2

Nyamata, 1998

The question of identity, allegiance, and being a Christian is not a speculative theological question. It is a concrete and urgent question, particularly in our time, living as we are after the 1994 Rwanda genocide. In less than a hundred days, close to a million Rwandans—mostly Tutsis—were killed by their neighbors and countrymen (mostly Hutus). The greatest irony of this genocide of our time is that it happened in one of the most Christianized countries in Africa, where at least 70 percent of the population

This essay was originally given as a lecture at the Catholicism Week, Center for World Catholicism and Intercultural Theology, De Paul University, Chicago, April 15, 2013. A revised version of the lecture was published as "Thinking Theologically about Identities and Allegiances: Parables of a 'New We,'" in *Beyond the Borders of Baptism: Catholicity, Allegiances, and Lived Identities*, ed. Michael L. Budde, ed. (Eugene, OR: Cascade Books, 2016). Reprinted with permission by the publishers.

was Catholic and 15 percent Protestant.[1] This means that almost all of the victims and their killers were Christians, who had been baptized and often worshipped in the same churches in which killings took place. The church of Nyamata was one such killing field. I visited the church of Nyamata in the summer of 1998, on my first visit to Rwanda after the genocide. Even though it had been four years since the genocide, the empty church carried fresh memories of what happened here. The corrugated tin roof was pierced by bullet holes and bore visible bloodstains; the church basement, accessible down steep steps in the back, had been converted into a permanent catacomb. On either side of its very narrow hallways were racks of skulls, bones, coffins, and personal belongings of the more than eight thousand people who had been killed inside the church. The expansive main area of the church was empty. The altar's white sheet covering still bore bloodstains. The tabernacle stood wide open; the marble baptismal font was chipped in a number of places, apparently by machetes intended for some of the victims.

As I stood in horrified silence in the empty church, a number of questions ran through my head. How could this have happened in this beautiful and deeply Christian country? Why was the Catholic Church never able to provide a bulwark against the slaughter of Rwandans by their neighbors, but was rather, as some cases indicated, a contributing factor in the killing?[2] The fact that the genocide started during Easter week added more irony and contradiction. For obviously, many of the victims had celebrated Christ's Resurrection from the dead, thus becoming the first fruit of God's new creation, here in this very church, together with the killers. Was all the talk of new identity, new life with God—

---

[1] Most accounts put the Christian population of Rwanda prior to the genocide between 85–90 percent. See, e.g., Carol Rittner, John K. Roth, and Wendy Wentworth, *Genocide in Rwanda: Complicity of the Churches?* (St. Paul, MN: Paragon House, 2004), xi; Timothy Longman, *Christianity and Genocide in Rwanda* (Cambridge: Cambridge University Press, 2011), 4. See also Emmanuel M. Katongole, "Christianity, Tribalism, and the Rwandan Genocide," *Logos: A Journal of Catholic Thought and Culture* 8, no. 3 (2005): 67–93.

[2] For some of these cases, see Emmanuel M. Katongole with Jonathan Wilson-Hartgrove, *Mirror to the Church: Resurrecting Faith after Genocide in Rwanda* (Grand Rapids, MI: Zondervan, 2009), esp. 9–26.

words that describe the life of the Christian—nothing but mere *spiritual* platitudes that actually meant very little in the "real" world? What, then, is the relationship between one's biological, national, racial, or ethnic identity and the reality of baptism? Does the blood of tribalism run deeper than the waters of baptism?

I begin with the vivid memory of Nyamata for two reasons. First, it is to make the point that a reflection about identity, allegiance, and being a Christian cannot proceed in an abstract fashion. It must always draw attention to a particular place (America, Africa, Rwanda—to the extent these notions are places) and begin by paying attention to the contradictions within which Christians find themselves as they engage the politics of their nations. But I also begin with the memory of Nyamata because it is now clear that what happened in Rwanda in 1994, while extreme and particularly intense, is by no means exceptional. For as Michael Budde notes, Christians readily kill other Christians in service to the claims of state, ethnicity, or ideology.[3] Moreover, such killing has become so commonplace that we no longer see this as a scandal to the Christian Gospel.[4] That is why Rwanda does serve well as a mirror—indeed, as a metaphor—for the modern forms of tribalism that habituate Christians to live in ways that assume that bonds of tribalism, nationalism, racism, or ethnicity run much deeper than the waters of baptism.[5] Accordingly, reflecting on Rwanda might provide us with much needed lessons for learning how to think theologically about identity and belonging in our time.

---

[3] Michael L. Budde, ed., *Beyond the Borders of Baptism: Catholicity, Allegiances, and Lived Identities* (Eugene, OR: Cascade Books, 2016).

[4] Ibid., 5. A key aspect of modern tribalism, as Budde describes, is that we have found ways to "explain away" the scandal of Christians killing other Christians: "World War I is described as interstate rivalry run amok, not the industrial butchering by Christians of one another; Rwanda symbolizes the ugliness of ethnic conflict rather than Catholics massacring Catholics; the U.S. wars in Central America are charged to the Cold War account instead of Christians in the United States abetting the killing of Nicaraguan, Salvadoran, and Guatemalan Christians by one another. That no one describes these events as a scandal to the gospel, a cruel inversion of the unity of the body of Christ, is among the most embarrassing charges against contemporary Christianity."

[5] I make this argument more explicitly in *Mirror to the Church*.

Learning to Think Theologically about Identity: The Dialectical Task

Learning to think theologically about identity involves two interrelated tasks, an intellectual task and a practical one. These interconnected tasks are nicely captured by Paul's words in his letter to the Romans, when he warns his audience: "Do not conform yourself to this age, but be transformed by the renewal of your mind, that you may discern what is the will of God, what is good and acceptable and perfect" (Rom 12:2).

Although in this essay I do not get into the historical, hermeneutical, and literary issues connected with Paul's letter to the Romans and this particular recommendation, what is clear is that, composed of both Jewish and Gentile Christians, the Church of Rome experienced some tensions. In writing this encouraging letter to the Romans, Paul highlights the new life of hope and freedom in Christ that God's love has given to all through God's unmerited justification. As bearers of this new life, Roman Christians must learn to think of themselves in a "new" way—not as Gentile and Jewish in the first place, but as God's new people, made such through God's unmerited grace. It is within this context that he urges them not to conform to this age but to live transformed lives. What is of particular significance for us here is the way that Paul suggests that Roman Christians might be able to go about the business of being transformed. They do so, according to Paul, in two interconnected ways. First, it is by the "renewal of your minds." What Paul recommends here is not a one-time "making up" of their minds, but a "renewal," which is to say an ongoing (trans)formation of their minds, which is realized through cultivation of the relevant habits of mind. The renewal of mind is about developing the necessary mental capacities and categories to enable them to think rightly—that is, in a manner consistent with their new status as God's people, made thus not through the law (the old categories) but through God's grace.

Second, Paul shows that learning to think rightly is not a detached intellectual exercise, even though it is about developing the right mental capacities and categories. Rather, it is connected to, and at the same time made possible by, relevant patterns of living. It is connected with the ability to "to discern what is the will of God, what is pleasing, perfect, and true." The key term here is "discern," which various translations render differently: so as "to test and approve what God's will is" (New International Version); "to learn and know God's will" (English Standard Version); "to prove what the will of God is" (New American Bible).

What the various translations confirm is the practical dimension of discernment as a form of living out the will of God: what is good, acceptable, and perfect. Moreover, if these different expressions ("test," "learn," "know," and "prove") seem to reflect a certain tentativeness in Paul's recommendation, they point to a crucial dimension of ad hoc discernment—experimentation, an ongoing negotiation of their new identity, which requires the formation of both relevant mental capacities and practical disciplines. These disciplines are at once as subversive (i.e., do not conform to the patterns of this world) as they are revelatory of what is good, pleasing, and perfect. Moreover, this way of understanding who they are and living in the world is a form of politics ("politics" here understood as the configuring of bodies in space and time).[6] That is why, in the end, thinking correctly about Christian identity is about learning to see one's body as both the site of resistance and the revelation of that new reality of God's justification. Thus, Paul states in the opening words of Romans 12, which immediately precede the exhortation not to conform to this age: "Therefore, I urge you, brothers and sisters, in view of God's mercy, to offer your bodies as a living sacrifice, holy and pleasing to God—this is your true and proper worship" (Rom 12:1 NIV).

This is what learning to think theologically about identity, allegiance, and being a Christian is about. But I realize I have jumped ahead of myself. My intention in drawing attention to Paul's exhortation to the Romans here was to highlight the two dialectical requirements of Christian identity: the cultivation of

---

[6]For this understanding of politics, see particularly William T. Cavanaugh, "The Church in the Streets: Eucharist and Politics," *Modern Theology* 30, no. 2 (2014): 384–402. For my response to, and a more extended discussion of, Cavanaugh's essay, see Emmanuel Katongole, "'A Blood Thicker than Tribalism': Eucharist and Identity in African Politics," *Modern Theology* 30, no. 2 (2014): 319–25.

relevant mental capacities and categories, on the one hand, and, on the other, the formation of relevant practical skills and postures that enable one to negotiate one's Christian identity in the world. Let me highlight each of these requirements by drawing some crucial lessons from the Rwanda genocide so as to provide more concrete and specific suggestions of what these might look like for us today.

Christian Identity as "Political" Identity

Rwanda forced me to rethink issues of ethnicity and nationalism and, overall, the status of so-called natural identities. The way the genocide in Rwanda was explained by Western media (and governments)—a myth that was reproduced throughout the world, including in Africa—was that the genocide in Rwanda was nothing but the playing out of age-old animosities between Tutsi and Hutu tribes or ethnicities. The impression of this pervasive explanation was that the Tutsi and Hutu were culturally and historically distinct communities, each with a different origin, and that they shared little in common other than their long-standing hatred for one another. This actually is not true. For not only did Hutu and Tutsi speak the same language, live on the same hills, intermarry, and intermingle, they also shared the same culture and the same religious traditions. In fact, prior to European colonialism, as Philip Gourevitch notes, "There are few people in Europe among whom one finds these three factors of national cohesion: one language, one faith, one law."[7]

What soon became clear through extended research on Rwanda was the fact that the categories of Hutu and Tutsi did not conform to the standard categories of race, tribe, or ethnicity, even though each of these had been subsequently used to describe Rwanda.[8] But what also became clear was that, even though Hutu and Tutsi continued to live on the same hills, speak the same language, and share the same cultural traditions, by 1994 Hutu and Tutsi had become two distinct and mutually exclusive

---

[7] Philip Gourevitch, *We Wish to Inform You That Tomorrow We Will Be Killed with Our Families: Stories from Rwanda* (New York: Picador, 1998), 55.

[8] See Emmanuel Katongole, *The Sacrifice of Africa: A Political Theology for Africa* (Grand Rapids, MI: Eerdmans, 2011), esp. 64–86.

"political" communities united by their hatred and fear of each other and their thirst for revenge. In particular, the work of the Ugandan Muslim scholar, Mahmood Mamdani, showed how Tutsi and Hutu had become political identities, produced and reproduced through the political formation of modern Rwanda by highlighting a crucial distinction between "cultural," "market," and "political" identities. Cultural identities reflect something of the past (a shared history, language, customs, beliefs, etc.); "political" identities are in view of a future political project (realizing specific political goals, or allocating access, privileges, etc.).[9]

Mamdani's conclusion—that Hutu and Tutsi did not merely reflect biological, racial, or cultural differences but rather were *formed* identities in view of particular political goals and aspirations—proved to be revolutionary for my thinking about identity. In the first place, it led me to see that there was something naively wrong in assuming that one's national, ethnic, or racial identity is one's "natural," and therefore, primary identity, on which one's being Christian builds. This rather widespread view is reflected in many ways, from assumptions that our "ethnicity" is the way God made us and nothing can be done about that,[10] to theological

---

[9]"We will need to distinguish political identity from both cultural and market based identities. Political identities exist in their own right. They are a direct consequence of the history of state formation, and not of market or cultural formation. If economic identities are a consequence of the history of development of markets, and cultural identities of the development of communities that share a common language and meaning, political identities need to be understood as a specific consequence of the history of state formation. When it comes to the modern state, political identities are inscribed in law. In the first instance, they are legally enforced" (Mahmood Mamdani, *When Victims Become Killers: Colonialism, Nativism, and the Genocide in Rwanda* [Oxford: James Currey, 2013], 22).

[10]See, e.g., Elie A. Buconyori, *Tribalism and Ethnicity* (Nairobi: AEA Theological and Christian Education Commission, 1997). The January 2009 Gathering of Christian Leaders in Reconciliation of the East African Great Lakes Initiative, organized by the Duke Center for Reconciliation and its partners in Bujumbura was titled "Identity, Community, and the Gospel of Reconciliation." Most leaders assumed as a starting point that the issue of ethnicity is a matter of biological givenness about which nothing can be done. The challenge, as many expressed it, was not "tribe" but "tribalism," which is considered to be exclusive concern for only one's tribe and hatred for anyone from another tribe. The gathering sought to show that the issue of tribalism was far more complex and often involves a call to live in a way that might involve "betraying" one's people. See Katongole, "Identity, Community and the Gospel of Reconciliation," the workbook for the 2009 Gathering, https://divinity.duke.edu.

arguments that invoke Aquinas's dictum that "grace builds upon nature" to suggest that Christian formation does not radically change or interrupt our natural identities, but simply builds on these.[11] But such formulations do not allow for the full political reality of Christian identity. For once it has been accepted that our biological, national, racial, or ethnic identities are our primary identities, then the best that Christianity might be able to do is to provide either inner spiritual dynamism to bolster those so-called natural identities or ethical guidelines to civilize and check the excessive tendencies of racism, tribalism, or nationalism. Christianity is left without any resources to question or interrupt the political goals and expectations toward which these so-called natural identities are directed.

That is why, in view of Mamdani's analysis, what became clear to me was that Christian identity is political identity—that is to say, it is a form of belonging that seeks to advance specific political visions of life and expectations. That is why the decisive practical and theological challenge has to do with clarity about the political ends ("the toward what?") of Christian identity, and then connected with that, of finding ways to realize these goals within the space of other contending political goals and expectations. It now became clear to me that, since Christians always finds

---

[11]I am aware, of course, that a great deal of African theological reflection was born out of an attempt to reclaim the African traditional heritage as a positive starting point—a veritable *praeparatio evangelica* for Christianity in Africa. African Christian theologians argued that African Christian identity does not start from a tabula rasa, but remains in continuity with (and thus builds on) the positive elements within the African Christian's traditional heritage. See, e.g., Kwame Bediako, *Theology and Identity: The Impact of Culture upon Christian Thought in the Second Century and in Modern Africa* (Eugene, OR: Wipf & Stock, 2011). Although I am greatly sympathetic to this historical moment of African theological reflection and applaud much of it—particularly the early contributions to the movement of African theology—my concern is that more recent contributions in the enculturation or indigenizing approach see the African heritage not simply as a "starting point," but as an end—the *terminus ad quem* of Christian identity. Thus, recent contributions seem to be more interested in merely dressing up Jesus in African garb—making Jesus simply one of us. For an extended critique of enculturation theology within the context of Rwanda, see Katongole, "Christianity, Tribalism, and the Rwandan Genocide." See also Emmanuel M. Katongole, "Of Faces of Jesus and *The Poisonwood Bible*," in *A Future for Africa: Critical Essays in Christian Social Imagination* (Scranton, PA: University of Scranton Press, 2005), 185–210.

themselves located within other forms of belonging (nation, race, ethnicity), which claim allegiance in pursuit of specific political goals and aims, it might be more useful to speak of Christian identity not in terms of a stable given or realized essence but as an ongoing journey that involves constant negotiation of existing political expectations and formations. Because of the prevailing tribalism through which Christians have become acculturated to live as though the bonds of race, tribe, nation, and ethnicity are more primary than the waters of baptism, a more specific conclusion was that Christian identity needs to be viewed as a form of "interruption," which will always have, in the words of Sam Wells, a "certain mischievous and subversive character"[12] within the existing political, national, ethnic, or racial formations. In view of this conclusion, I saw the contemporary urgency of Paul's exhortation to the Romans, which I began to paraphrase thus:

> *Brothers and sisters, do not be naïve about the politics of your nations; do not just fit within the forms of belonging as defined by your race, ethnicity, nationality or class, but be transformed by the renewing of your minds, so that you learn to negotiate what is perfect, true, and good.*

Negotiating Christian Identity: Parables of a "New We"

God is determined to form a new people in the world. Baptism and the entire range of Christian practice are meant to reflect and to advance this political reality. Although in this essay I cannot pursue a full explication of this claim, by describing God's purpose as "political," I want to make clear that the Kingdom of God is not merely a "spiritual" reality (that dwells within the interiority of the Christian conscience) or a mystical reality that wafts above the concrete forms of everyday life and belonging. It

---

[12]Samuel Wells, *Improvisation: The Drama of Christian Ethics* (Grand Rapids, MI: Brazos Press, 2004), 19. In this book, Sam Wells uses the notion of drama and performance to depict Christian life. Using Sam Wells's characterization in this context might suggest that we learn to view Christian baptism as a note or tune—somewhat off-key and even jarring given its strangeness—whose goal is not simply to "interrupt" the well-rehearsed symphonies of cultural and national identities but rather to reframe and point these compositions within a totally different telos, thus creating a new musical composition and performance.

is a real, concrete form of being in the world, of which the church is a sacrament. As a sacrament, the church is both the visible representation (a kind of "demonstration plot") as well as a sign of (and thus only points to) the full reality that is yet to come. Given this sacramental nature, it is perhaps not surprising that, in the Gospels, Jesus speaks about the Kingdom of God using parables.[13] Accordingly, since Christian identity is in view of the politics of the Kingdom of God, it calls for parables that are able not only to capture its reality in our time but also to illumine the opportunities and possibilities, and the tactics and skills, that are needed to negotiate the practical and social requirements of Christian identity in the context of other forms of belonging in the world. In the remaining sections of this essay, I suggest four such parables.

Ephesian Moments of a "New We"

God is determined to form a new people in the world. Christian identity seeks to create, realize, and reflect "Ephesian moments" of this movement of God in the world. Paul writes that God's purpose in Christ was to create, out of many, "one new man" (Eph 2:15), so that Jewish and Gentile Christians now share "one Spirit" (2:18), "one hope" (4:4), "one Lord, one faith, one baptism, [as they are all children of] one God and Father of all" (4:5–6). For Paul, these are not simply spiritual platitudes but concrete possibilities that the Christians of Ephesus have already began to experience and live out. Accordingly, Andrew Walls, the famed historian of world Christianity, rightly notes that the original Ephesian moment was the coming together for the first time of Jewish and Gentile Christians. It is this coming together of two

---

[13]For Jesus, using parables was at once a modality of communication—a form of analogy, through which he tried to capture a reality that was here and yet not here—and a form of social critique. In this sense, the focus of Jesus' parables was not only a vision of the reign of God but also the gory details of the dominant structures that obscured and resisted the reign of God. For this understanding of Jesus' parables, see, e.g., William R. Hertzog, *Parables as Subversive Speech: Jesus as Pedagogue of the Oppressed* (Louisville, KY: Westminster, 1994). In line with Hertzog, I use "parables" here as both a form of social analysis and a form of theological reflection, as both an exercise in teleological exposition and of social critique.

communities historically separated—the breaking down of the wall of separation brought about by Christ's death (2:13–18)—that Paul celebrates in his letter to the Ephesians. Jewish and Gentile Christians are "no longer strangers and sojourners, but . . . fellow citizens" and "members of God's household" (2:19). Thus, if the letter to the Ephesians recognizes the cultural and political realities of being Jew and Gentile, this is not what Paul celebrates, but rather the fact of their "coming together"—of their being "made alive" together (2:5), of being raised up together, sitting together (2:6). Jewish and Gentile Christians "belong together" as "bricks—used in the construction of a single building—the temple where the One God would live" (2:19–22). They do not constitute two separate communities but one community, of which they are both members, constituting as it were (and now Paul uses another image: the body) different parts of a single body of which "Christ is the head, the mind, the brain, under whose control the whole body works and is held together" (4:15–16).[14]

Three elements of Walls's description of the original Ephesian moment speak directly to an appreciation of Christian identity. First, involved in the Ephesian moment is the realization that, on their own, Jewish and Gentile Christians remain but "fragments" of God's purpose. Together—and only together—can the fragments come to the "very height of Christ's full stature." Thus, on our own—as American, Asian, African, white, black, etc., Christians—we remain but "fragments." It is only by coming together that these different fragments reflect the church's maturity—the very height of Christ's full stature. Second, and connected with this observation, is the realization that the coming together of Jewish and Gentile Christians creates something new. "The full height of Christ's full stature" that Paul celebrates is about this new and odd communion of believers that is neither Jewish nor Gentile. This is what is going on at Antioch, where the term "Christian" was first used. In a unique Ephesian moment, Jews and Gentiles came together. Their coming together created a "new we" that required a new name. No one had needed such a term when they existed independently as only Jew and Gentile. Third,

---

[14]Andrew F. Walls, "The Ephesian Moment: At a Crossroads in Christian History," in Andrew F. Walls, *The Cross-Cultural Process in Christian History* (Maryknoll, NY: Orbis Books, 2002), 77.

as Walls notes, the expression and test of that coming together was the meal table: "Two cultures historically separated by the meal table were now able to come together at table to share the knowledge of Christ."[15] Thus, the meal table—the institution that had once symbolized the ethnic and cultural division—now became the hallmark of Christian living. It is this experience that was reproduced at Antioch, Jerusalem, and other places as "one of the most noticeable features of life in the Jesus community," for "the followers of Jesus took every opportunity to eat together."[16]

An appreciation of Christian identity in our time requires creating and finding opportunities for eating together across national, racial, tribal, and ethnic boundaries. It is these opportunities of eating together that not only "break down the dividing walls of hostility" but also create forms of catholicity that reflect and reveal something of the "very height of Christ's full stature." It is something of the Ephesian moment that is glimpsed in the story of Father André Sibomana, who narrowly survived the genocide in Rwanda. In the aftermath of the genocide, he mobilized Christians for the reconstruction of schools, public places, and houses for genocide survivors. The Christians were both Hutu and Tutsi. At the beginning, the Hutu and Tutsi did not speak to one another. But the communal work helped build bridges. At the inauguration of the first two hundred houses on August 21, 2005, Hutu and Tutsi drank banana beer from the same jug.[17]

The Future Is Mestizo

Christian identity presses toward a mestizo[18] existence. Nobody has captured this reality as well as Father Virgilio Elizondo. "The core of our existence," Elizondo writes, "is to be other," to embrace a "new identity"; it is to live "in between" cultures—nei-

---

[15]Ibid., 78.

[16]Ibid., 77.

[17]André Sibomana et al., *Hope for Rwanda: Conversations with Laure Guilbert and Hervé Deguine* (London: Pluto Press, 1999), 131–32.

[18]*Mestizo* is a Spanish word that was first used to describe the children of the violent encounter between European fathers and Amerindian mothers; neither European nor Indian, these children belonged to a new people, a people of mixed heritage. See Virgilio P. Elizondo, *The Future Is Mestizo: Where Life and Cultures Meet* (Boulder: University Press of Colorado, 2000).

ther this nor that but fully both,[19] always straining ("journeying") toward the fuller reality of a new humanity that Jesus himself represents. Speaking of his own hyphenated life as a Mexican American and what that has taught him about the Christian identity, Elizondo writes, "Mestizo are part of both while not being exclusively either":

> Yet in neither am I ever considered one of the group. I am always both kin (at home) and foreigner at the same time. This "in-between" is the pain and the potential, the suffering and the joy, the confusion and the mystery, the darkness and the light of Mestizo life. As I claim this ambiguity and recognize it for what it truly is, I become the bearer of a new civilization that is inclusive of all the previous ones. No longer do I carry the burden of the shameful news, but rather become the bearer of the good news of the future that has already begun in us.[20]

This in-between, far from being negative, has tremendous advantage:

> I am an insider-outsider of both and thus have the ability of knowing both from within and from the outside. . . . I can know them in ways that they can never know me or suspect. I can truly become the interlocutor who will help both to see and appreciate themselves and each other in ways they have never before suspected.[21]

Even more significantly, Elizondo notes that mestizo is, by its very nature and origin, a radical transvaluation (to use a Nietzschean term) of all biological, cultural, and political categories as "the mestizo 'in-between' keeps expanding as the 'frontera' keeps expanding both north and south at the same time; it keeps including more and more peoples, more ethnicities, and races."[22]

It is this future as mestizo, as "in-between" that is glimpsed

---

[19]Ibid., 26.
[20]Ibid., 129.
[21]Ibid.
[22]Ibid., 128–29.

in the story of the confused Hutu boy who, during the Rwanda genocide, fled to the bush with the Tutsis. After two or three weeks, the Tutsis pointed out to him that he was Hutu and so could be saved. He left the marshes and was not attacked. But the mixed-up boy had spent so much time with Tutsis in his early childhood that he was confused. He didn't know how to draw the "proper" line between ethnic groups. Afterward, when he returned to his village, he did not get involved in the killings. The *interahammwe* militias tried to force him to participate in the killing but eventually gave up on him because his mind was, in their words, "clearly overwhelmed."[23] The challenge and invitation of Christian identity in our time is about forming such confused, overwhelmed, mestizo Christians.

Ecclesial Solidarity

Negotiating Christian identity in our time requires Christians to pursue a radical form of solidarity that cuts across national, racial, ethnic, and cultural boundaries. Among other things, this means that Christians need to understand our membership in the Body of Christ as our primary identity. I find Michael Budde's characterization of this notion of "ecclesial solidarity" quite illuminating. Christians, Budde writes, need to think of themselves as joined first and foremost to one another, and only secondarily, or derivatively, to other corporate claimants on their affections and allegiances.

> When Christians take ecclesial solidarity as their starting point for discernment—political, economic, liturgical, and otherwise—it makes them members of a community broader than the largest nation-state, more pluralistic than any culture in the world, more deeply rooted in the lives of the poor and marginalized than any revolutionary movement, more capable of exemplifying the notion of *e pluribus unum* than any empire past, present, or future. Seeing oneself as a member of the worldwide body of Christ invites communities to join their local stories to other stories of sin

---

[23]Katongole, *Mirror to the Church*, 45–46.

and redemption, sacrifice and martyrdom, rebellion and forgiveness unlike any other on offer via allegiance to one's tribe, gendered movements, or class fragment.[24]

That the suggestion of ecclesial identity as primary identity may today strike many as strange just goes to confirm the extent to which modern political allegiances have succeeded to fragment the body of Christ along national, racial, and ethnic forms of belonging, thereby helping perpetuate the "spiritualization" of Christian baptism and identity, and making it impossible to counteract the reproduction of tribalism in its many current forms. This development, however, is a recent (modern) one. For, as Budde notes,

> The earliest Christians would have found nothing exceptional in the idea of "ecclesial solidarity." Early Christians saw themselves, and were seen by others, as more than just a new "religious" group, more than a new idea unleashed in the ancient world, and more than a voluntary club like other social groupings of association. . . . Early Christians were more often seen as part of a new ethnic group, even a new race of people, in the Roman World.[25]

Moreover, what was unique about this new race was the way in which it was able not only to redefine Roman notions of race as fixed identity but also to demonstrate that becoming part of this new race or ethnic community was available to all regardless of their communities or identities of origin. "Conversion" was the process through which one became a member of this new race. That is why, within this context, conversion is best seen "not as a private matter of individual conscience resulting in an individual's affiliation with a religious movement, but explicitly as becoming a member of a people, with collective and public consequences."[26]

It is this kind of "solidarity"—membership into a new people, drawn from but much deeper than any nation, race, tribe, or ethnicity—that is glimpsed in the story of the Muslim Nyami-

---

[24]Budde, *Beyond the Borders of Baptism*, 4.

[25]Ibid., 7. See also Denise Kimber Buell, *Why This New Race? Ethnic Reasoning in Early Christianity* (New York: Columbia University Press, 2008), 2–3.

[26]Budde, *Beyond the Borders of Baptism*, 8.

rambo community. In his account of the Rwanda genocide, Gérard Prunier contrasts the widespread involvement of Christian
churches in the genocide with the case of the Muslim community
at the outskirts of Kigali: "The only community that was able to
provide a bulwark against barbarity for its adherents was Islam.
There are many testimonies to the protection of members the
Muslim community gave each other, and their refusal to divide
themselves ethnically."[27] There might have been many reasons for
the solidarity that this community exhibited. One reason I find
particularly telling is quite powerful in illuminating the ecclesial
solidarity that being a Christian ought to be about, but at which
the church often fails. The solidarity of the Muslim community,
Prunier notes, came from the fact that "being Muslim in Rwanda,
where Muslims are a very small (0.2 percent) proportion of the
population, is not simply a choice dictated by religion: it is a
global identity choice. Muslims are often marginal people and
this reinforces a strong sense of community identification, which
supersedes ethnic tags, something the majority Christians have
not been able to achieve."[28]

A Living Sacrifice

Negotiating Christian identity calls for postures of resistance
against modern forms of tribalism and therefore the willingness
to offer one's body as a "living sacrifice." In the opening words
of the section of Paul's letter to the Romans already cited, Paul
appeals to the Romans: "Therefore, I urge you, brothers and
sisters, in view of God's mercy, to offer your bodies as a living
sacrifice, holy and pleasing to God—this is your true and proper
worship" (Rom 12:1). It is this kind of courage and sacrifice to
which the story of Sister Félicité Niyitegeka of Gisenyi bears witness. A Hutu nun aged about sixty, Sister Félicité Niyitegeka was
the director of an orphanage, the Centre Sainte Pierre in Gisenyi.
She sheltered refugees during the genocide. When her brother, a
colonel in the Rwandan army, instructed her to leave to escape
being killed, she wrote the following letter to him:

---

[27]Gérard Prunier, *The Rwanda Crisis: History of a Genocide* (London: Hurst,
2010), 253.
[28]Ibid.

Thank you for wanting to help me. I would rather die than abandon the forty-three persons for whom I am responsible. Pray for us, that we may come to God. Say "goodbye" to our old mother and our brother. When I come to God, I shall pray for you. Keep well. Thank you for thinking of me. If God saves us, as we hope, we shall see you tomorrow. Yours, Sr. Félicité Niyitegeka.[29]

Sister Félicité and her sisters continued to shelter refugees and save others by helping them across the borders. When the militia arrived on April 21, they transported the remaining Tutsis together with Sister Félicité and her sisters to an already prepared mass grave. They shot to death more than twenty refugees and six of the sisters, leaving Sister Félicité for last. "I have no reason to live," she said, "now that you have killed all my sisters." The militia leader asked her to pray for him before he shot her.

It is stories like these that point to what it means to think theologically about identity, allegiance, and being a Christian, which, as my analysis here shows, is about learning to live in a way that defies tribalism in its many forms. The stories illumine the form and shape of Christian baptism as incorporation into a new social reality, a new form of belonging to a community that extends beyond boundaries of time and geography and of ethnicity, race, and nationality, and even beyond terrestrial and celestial boundaries. For it was only by locating herself as a member of this "new we" that includes those who have already gone before us, that Sister Félicité was willing to offer her body, knowing that her life is not wasted but is gathered up, as a fragrant offering, a living sacrifice holy and pleasing to God. That she willingly accepted death rather than surrender the refugees is an indication that, throughout her life, in her calling and serving, she was able to understand herself as already a member of that immense crowd, the "multitude that no one could count, drawn from every nation, tribe, people, and language, standing before the throne and

---

[29]Aylward Shorter, *Christianity and the African Imagination: Resources for Inculturation* (Nairobi: Paulines, 1996), 13. See also James Martin, *This Our Exile: A Spiritual Journey with the Refugees of East Africa* (Maryknoll, NY: Orbis Books, 2011), 188.

before the Lamb" (Rev 7:9). Her story, just like the other stories, is both the argument and evidence that Christian identity is not merely a mystical or spiritual reality, but a concrete, historical, and social reality that has been made possible through the death and resurrection of Christ. Moreover, these stories or parables point to what it means—and how exactly one might be able—to heed Paul's exhortation to the Roman Christians: "Do not conform yourself to this age, but be transformed by the renewal of your mind, that you may discern what is the will of God, what is good and acceptable and perfect." Only by developing the relevant mental capacities and categories and the concomitant skills of living in the world in a manner consistent with our new identity as God's new people might we be able to resist the pervasive forms of modern tribalism, for which the Rwanda genocide is a metaphor, and thus show that the waters of baptism run deeper that the blood of tribalism.

6

On Learning to Betray One's People

The Gospel and a Culture of Peace in Africa

The question of the authentic experience and expression of Christian faith continues to be the most pressing theological and missiological question of our time, particularly in Africa. However, whereas the quest has, since the 1960s, been dominated by questions of the relation of Christian faith to African culture,[1] we now find ourselves in a radically different context, one in which the question of the authenticity of Christian faith in Africa must be seen in light of the political violence that threatens much of postcolonial Africa. In our time, the primary challenge facing the majority of Christians in Africa is not whether or how to relate

---

This essay was originally given as the Luzbetak Lecture in Mission and Culture, Catholic Theological Union, Chicago, September 29, 2014. I am grateful to Father Stephen Bevans for the invitation to deliver the lecture and the permission to publish it here in this collection.

[1] For this preoccupation within African theology, see, e.g., Justin S. Upkong, "The Emergence of African Theology," *Theological Studies* 45 (1984) 501–536; John S. Mbiti, *New Testament Eschatology in an African Background: A Study of the Encounter between New Testament Theology and African Traditional Concepts* (London: Oxford University Press, 1971); Charles Nyamiti, *Christ as Our Ancestor: Christology in an African Perspective* (Zimbabwe: Mambo Press, 1984); Robert J. Schreiter, ed., *Faces of Jesus in Africa* (Maryknoll, NY: Orbis Books, 1991); Benezet Bujo, *African Theology in its Social Context* (Maryknoll, NY: Orbis Books, 1992).

one's faith to one's culture, but whether the Christian faith can offer resources for peaceful coexistence in the context of widespread conflict and war. Given the endless cycles of violence, African Christians are right to wonder if their Christian faith makes any difference, and if so, what kind of difference.

I argue that Christianity does indeed make a difference, but that for Christian faith to offer a radical interruption to the cycles of violence in Africa, it has to be grounded within an explicit missiological vision of "Ephesian" identities and communities. The story of the forty young students of Buta provides a most illuminating example of Ephesian community. In the early hours of the morning in the autumn of 1997, a militia group, headed by a fierce woman commander, attacked Buta, a high school seminary in Burundi. They roused the students from their sleep and ordered them to separate, Hutu on one side and Tutsi on the other. Three times the order was given, but the students refused to stand apart. The commander then ordered the rebels to open fire. Students fell, and those left standing tried to escape. In all, forty students were killed. One of the students who had been wounded ran to the rector's house, and called for the rector to open the door for him. When the rector opened the door, the boy dashed inside the small house, and gasping for breath said: "Father, we have won. They told us to separate and we refused. We have won." Then he collapsed and died.[2]

I want to look at that "we have won." For it is the logic of this odd "winning" and the practices that made it possible that missiological reflection in Africa must increasingly be about given the context of political violence. The essay proceeds in two parts. First, I narrate political violence as a unique theological problem in Africa. I do so by reflecting on three key scholarly insights from the 1994 Rwanda genocide, whose overall impact has been to press for fresh theological and missiological approaches in African Christianity. Second, using the work of Andrew Walls, I propose a missiological framework within which the realities of political violence in Africa can be fruitfully engaged. Andrew Walls's work helps show that the goal of mission is essentially

---

[2]Author interview with Father Zachary Bukuru, who was rector at the time of the attack, Buta, August 13, 2009.

political; that is, the formation of "Ephesian" communities whose identity supersedes ethnic tags and thus reflects the "very height of Christ's full stature." Such Ephesian communities provide the most decisive interruption and alternative to the violent politics of race, ethnicity, and tribalism. The seminary at Buta in Burundi was such a community. By narrating the practices that formed this community, I illumine the logic and practices through which the Gospel shapes a culture of peace in Africa.

Rwanda 1994: Political Violence as a Theological and Missiological Problem

The 1994 Rwanda genocide not only changed the trajectory of my scholarship, it led me to see political violence as a theological problem in Africa and the kind of theological problem it is. I was in Belgium, starting research on a PhD in philosophy at KULeuven, when the Rwanda genocide took place in the spring of 1994. As I watched the television images of thousands of dead bodies in the streets, hills, rivers, and churches in Rwanda, I was at once filled with a sense of shame, anguish, and disbelief. The experience raised a number of questions in my mind. On a personal level, they were questions about my own history and identity. Who was I? Was I Ugandan, or Rwandan, Hutu or Tutsi? And what is identity? Is it always an either-or? [3] Other questions related to my African heritage. The Rwanda genocide was a very intimate affair, often carried out by machetes and other farm instruments, with relatives killing relatives, neighbors killing neighbors. But how could people who shared so much in common kill one another? What about those quintessential African virtues of hospitality, community, family, and brotherhood, which John Mbiti nicely summed up as the true expression of African

---

[3]These were not academic or abstract questions for me. My parents had been born and raised in Rwanda, one Hutu and one Tutsi, whereas I myself was born in Uganda. These questions of identity have continued to be a crucial factor shaping my work and scholarship, which is always (it seems to me) at the intersection of multiple locations, stories, identities, and traditions. For an extended reflection on the question of multiple belongings and its theological, existential, and methodological implications, see my "A Tale of Many Stories," in *Shaping a Global Theological Mind*, ed. Darren C. Marks (Burlington, VT: Ashgate, 2008), 89–94.

identity: "I am because we are and since we are therefore I am."[4] Watching the expatriation of Western nationals, effectively abandoning millions of helpless Rwandans to the murderous brutality of the Interahamwe militias, raised yet another set of questions concerning claims about a common humanity. Was there any such thing as a "human community," or was that simply a platitude and a mask behind calculated national self-interest?[5] However, perhaps by far the more disturbing questions were related to the realization that Rwanda was an overwhelmingly Christian county, one in which Catholics made up more than 80 percent of the population. That the Christian churches where the majority of Rwandans worshipped became killing fields during the genocide raised fundamental questions about mission. How could Christians kill one another, often within the same churches they worshipped in? Is the blood of tribalism deeper than the waters of baptism? The fact that the genocide unfolded during Holy Week made the question even more poignant.[6]

On a scholarly level, the Rwanda genocide had a number of immediate and long-time impacts. First, in the wake of the genocide there was a sense of the utter irrelevance and even uselessness of my scholarly pursuit. Here I was doing a doctorate in philosophy (and studying interesting figures like Hegel, Habermas, and Heidegger), and there were my brothers and sisters killing each other in the name of ethnicity. The long-term effect of this desolation was a nagging question about not simply my own studies, but about scholarship in general, especially as it relates to Africa. For I was beginning to get a feeling that unless my academic pursuit was able to shed light on events like this, which threatened the very foundations of social existence in Africa, it was totally useless and in fact a distraction. But the issue was beyond my own scholarship, for in the wake of genocide, I was beginning to form

---

[4]John Mbiti, *African Religions and Philosophy* (Garden City, NY: Anchor Books, 1970).

[5]On the betrayal of Rwanda by Western powers, see particularly Linda Melvern, *A People Betrayed: The Role of the West in Rwanda's Genocide* (London: Zed Books, 2000). See also Roméo Dallaire, *Shake Hands with the Devil: The Failure of Humanity in Rwanda* (Cambridge, MA: Da Capo Press, 2005).

[6]For an extended theological reflection on this, see my "Violence and Christian Social Reconstruction in Africa: On the Resurrection of the Body (Politic)," *Other Journal,* August 8, 2005, http://theotherjournal.com.

the conviction that scholarly pursuit must be missional; even more specifically, it must be connected to the search for a future beyond war, violence, and genocide. Looking back, I realize that it must have been this conviction that led me to focus my research on understanding the role of violence in political history, and on the power of stories in shaping political imagination. My decision to enroll in a part-time Master's program in religious studies, so as to get a better sense of the logic of Christian ethics, must also somehow have been driven by these convictions that were shaping me in the wake of the genocide.

Since I completed my doctorate in 1996, my scholarly engagement has continued to be shaped by the Rwanda genocide. Consequently, I have made and led a number of pilgrimages[7] to Rwanda, taught courses, and published on the genocide. Out of this ongoing engagement, three crucial insights have emerged. First, a clear sense that the genocide was not a form of "ethnic" or tribal violence but a unique form of *political* violence. As the genocide unfolded, the standard explanation was that what was playing out in Rwanda was nothing but "age-old animosities" between Tutsi and Hutu tribes. Such an explanation assumes that "Tutsi" and "Hutu" are culturally and historically distinct communities, each with a distinct origin. But this is not true. For whatever role the categories of Hutu and Tutsi played in precolonial Rwanda, they cannot be reasonably referred to as "tribes" or "ethnicities." For not only did Hutu and Tutsi speak the same language, they shared the same culture, same religious traditions, lived on the same hills, and were greatly intermarried. And, as noted in the previous chapter, "there are few people in Europe among whom one finds these three factors of national cohesion: one language, one faith, one law."[8]

As noted previously, the work of the Ugandan scholar Mahmood Mamdani led me to see that Hutu and Tutsi did not reflect

---

[7]On pilgrimage as a unique form of mission engagement, see my "From Tower Dwellers to Travelers," interview by Andy Crouch, *Christianity Today*, July 3, 2007: http://www.christianitytoday.com. See also my "Mission and the Ephesian Moment of World Christianity: Pilgrimages of Pain and Hope and the Economics of Eating Together," *Mission Studies* 29, no. 2 (2012): 183–200.

[8]Philip Gourevitch, *We Wish to Inform You That Tomorrow We Will Be Killed with Our Families: Stories from Rwanda* (New York: Picador, 1998), 55.

biological, racial, or cultural differences. Rather, they were *po-litical* identities, which were formed and reproduced within the political history of Rwanda. In *When Victims Become Killers*, Mamdami makes a helpful distinction between "cultural," and "political" identities. Cultural identities reflect something of the past (a shared history, language, customs, beliefs, etc.), whereas "political" identities are in view of a future political project:

> They are a direct consequence of the history of state forma-tion, and not of market or cultural formation. If economic identities are a consequence of the history of development of markets, and cultural identities of the development of communities that share a common language and meaning, political identities need to be understood as a specific con-sequence of the history of state formation. When it comes to the modern state, political identities are inscribed in law. In the first instance, they are legally enforced.[9]

This distinction helps explain why even though Hutu and Tutsi continued to live on the same hills, speak the same language, and share the same cultural traditions, by 1994 Hutu and Tutsi had become two distinct and mutually exclusive "political" com-munities united by their hatred and fear of each other and thirst for revenge. That they had become so is the work of political imagination. Thus, Mamdani is able to show how the Belgian colonial regime was able, using the Hamitic story to theorize the categories of Hutu and Tutsi as "racial" identities reflecting distinct origins and capabilities, the Hamitic race (Tutsi) being more advanced than the negroid (Hutu) population. And that by making them the stable, unquestionable building blocks of the modern state of Rwanda, the colonial regime helped reinforce and reproduce these identities, a process that continued after independence. And so, while the Habyerimana regime succeeded in redefining the identities as "ethnic" (and not "racial"), it never questioned the theory of distinct origins nor the mythology that "constant warfare" is what had always existed between the two

---

[9]Mahmood Mamdani, *When Victims Become Killers: Colonialism, Nativism, and the Genocide in Rwanda* (Princeton, NJ: Princeton University Press, 2001), 22.

groups. The 1994 genocide was by and large the unfolding of this *political* imagination.

The second insight that has emerged in my ongoing research on Rwanda is the fact that by locating itself neatly within the political imagination of Rwanda, Christian mission was able to become at once "successful" but politically impotent. That this is the case is confirmed by the fact that even though Christianity had become an integral part of the social, political, and cultural history of Rwanda, when it came to the 1994 genocide, Christianity made no significant difference. On the contrary, during the genocide, Christians were at best bystanders, at worst participants in the killing. That Christianity was not able to provide any bulwark against genocide, as is now obvious, has partly to do with the way Christian mission allied itself neatly with the colonial project of building a modern Rwanda nation-state. Missionaries not only took for granted but were enamored by the anthropology and science of races that became the basis for the political imagination of Rwanda.[10] Accordingly, Christian mission never sought to provide an alternative imaginary, along different anthropological lines, for Rwandan society. On the contrary, as Mamdani notes, "when it came to breathe institutional life into the Hamitic hypothesis, the colonial church acted as both the brains and hands of the colonial state. In this instance, at least the church did both the strategic thinking and the dirty work for the state."[11]

But this limitation of mission, the inability to question, let alone crack open, the political imagination of society based on the notions of race, tribe, and ethnicity must also be understood against the background of the nineteenth-century Christian missionary enterprise in general. Shaped within an Enlightenment context, nineteenth-century missionary work by and large as-

---

[10]The sentiments of the missionary Louis de Lacger (remarking that the contrast between the plurality of the races of Rwanda was possibly the most fascinating part of the country) and of Monsignor Leon Classe, the first bishop of Rwanda (warning that any effort to replace "the wellborn" Tutsi chiefs with "uncouth" Hutus would lead the entire state into anarchy) were greatly shared by other missionaries. (See Gourevitch, *We Wish to Inform You*, 54–56.) For a nuanced reading of these missionary attitudes toward the races, see James Carney, *Rwanda before the Genocide: Catholic Politics and Ethnic Discourse in Late Colonial Era* (Oxford: Oxford University Press, 2014).

[11]Mamdani, *When Victims Become Killers*, 99.

sumed and operated out of a neo-Scholastic grace versus nature distinction according to which mission (the church's competence) was located within an essentially "spiritual" realm, thus surrendering the "natural" sphere to the realm of politics. And thus, even when evangelization met with great success, as the case of Rwanda confirms, it was simply assumed that the church's role was primarily spiritual and pastoral. Accordingly, the church never understood itself as competent or even able to provide an alternative configuration of Rwandan society in terms of a distinct Christian anthropology beyond the notions of Hutu and Tutsi, which had by now come to be accepted as natural identities. The legacy of this mission heritage is evident not only in Rwanda but in sub-Saharan Africa in general, where Christianity largely operates within a self-policed spiritual and religious sphere, which in effect surrenders the so-called natural sphere to the realm of politics. But by locating itself within this spiritual mold, Christianity not only sustains a misleading assumption that it does not have a unique anthropology or sociology into which it seeks to invite Christians, it also allows politics and the field of secular anthropology to have a final say in what African society is or can become. The overall effect of this religious outlook of Christianity is not only an exaggerated deference to the so-called natural categories of race, tribe, or ethnicity, it is to seal off these notions from the possibility of any radical theological reconfiguration.[12] This is what turns these so-called natural identities into rich fodder for ideological manipulation within the violent politics of postcolonial Africa.

The third crucial insight that was to emerge in the wake of the 1994 Rwanda genocide was the shocking realization that the genocide was not an exception—it represented a radicalization of a regular feature of modern African politics. This should perhaps not be surprising in view of the foregoing observations. But it did come as a fresh insight that a similar political imagination grounded in ethnicity and the mythology of constant warfare was at work in many African societies, and that, just as in Rwanda,

---

[12]For more on this, see my "'A Blood Thicker than the Blood of Tribalism': Eucharist and Identity in African Politics," *Modern Theology* 30, no. 2 (2014): 319–25.

Christianity seems unable to provide any bulwark against the political violence in these countries. That this is so is confirmed by a number of cases.

The Congo Wars, as they have now come to be known, have claimed over 5.6 million lives.[13] It has been estimated that as many as 3.3 million people died just in the Second War (1996–2003), which has been described by the International Rescue Committee (IRC) as "the most deadly war ever documented on African soil with the highest death toll anywhere in the world since World War II."[14] A key development in this war was the "Ituri conflict," which pitted Hema against Lendu communities. Not unlike Rwanda, the fact that Hema and Lendu had lived together and extensively intermarried, or that both were largely Christian, did not seem to make much difference in the large-scale massacres perpetrated by members of both ethnic groups against the other.[15]

More recently, the developments in the Central African Republic (CAR) have captured the world's attention. In March 2013, violence broke out after Seleka rebels—loosely organized groups that drew primarily Muslim fighters from other countries—ousted the president (Bozize) and installed their own leader. Even though the Seleka were subsequently disbanded, its members continued to commit crimes such as pillaging, looting, rape, and murder. In response, Antibalaka self-defense groups began to form and soon the conflict in the nation took on a sectarian character, as some Antibalaka, many of whom are Christian (80 percent of CAR's 4.5 million people are Christians), began attacking Muslims out

---

[13]For a good introduction, see Thomas Turner, *The Congo Wars: Conflict, Myth and Reality* (London: Zed Books, 2007); see also Gérard Prunier, *Africa's World War: Congo, the Rwanda Genocide, and the Making of a Continental Catastrophe* (Oxford: Oxford University Press, 2008). On the social and human dynamics and costs of the wars, see particularly Jason K. Stearns, *Dancing in the Glory of Monsters: The Collapse of the Congo and the Great War of Africa* (New York: Public Affairs, 2012).

[14]International Rescue Committee, *Special Report: Congo,* 2003.

[15]A helpful starting point in getting a sense of the ethnic complexities in the Second Congo War is Johan Pottier's "Representations of Ethnicity in the Search for Peace: Ituri, Democratic Republic of Congo," *African Affairs* 109, no. 434 (2010): 23–50, http://afraf.oxfordjournals.org. See also Mahmood Mamdani, "The Invention of the Indigène," *London Review of Books* 33, no. 2 (January 20, 2011): 31–33, http://www.lrb.co.uk.

of revenge for the Seleka's acts. As of May 2014, more than 2,000 people had been killed, a million people displaced, with reports warning of possible genocide.[16]

South Sudan, which gained independence from Sudan in July 2011 as the outcome of a 2005 peace deal that ended Africa's longest-running civil war, is yet another case. In December 2013, the young state plunged into crisis amid a power struggle between President Salva Kiir and his deputy, Riek Machar, whom he had sacked. The crisis soon turned into an ethnic civil war between members of Kiir's ethnic Dinka community and Machar's Nuer group. The death toll has now risen to over 10,000, with over 800,000 displaced, and reports warning of possible genocide.[17]

Many social, historical, and geopolitical factors can explain each of these complex conflicts. What cannot be denied, however, is the readiness with which political conflict in Africa generates into "ethnic" conflict. Elsewhere I have argued that the notions of "ethnicity" and "tribe" are wired within the imaginative landscape of modern Africa, making "ethnic conflict" not only a perpetual feature of postcolonial Africa, but "ethnicity" as an enduring and readily available tool for political mobilization.[18] What I hope this brief analysis makes clear is that these so-called ethnic wars or conflicts are not so much about irreconcilable ethnic or cultural differences,[19] but are about a struggle and competition for power by the elite, into which ethnicity easily gets invoked and reproduced. From a missiological point of view what one finds disturbing is how little difference the fact of being a Christian seems to make. It is in this regard that Rwanda is not simply an example, but a

---

[16] *World Post*, May 6, 2014.

[17] Statistics as of May 2014. See Alastair Leithead, "John Kerry Warns of South Sudan Genocide," *BBC News Africa*, May 1, 2014, at http://www.bbc.com.

[18] See my *The Sacrifice of Africa: A Political Theology for Africa* (Grand Rapids, MI: Eerdmans, 2011), esp. 64–86.

[19] In this connection, see also the interesting work by Stuart Kaufman, *Modern Hatreds: The Symbolic Politics of Ethnic War* (Ithaca, NY: Cornell University Press, 2001). Kaufman argues that ethnic war is a modern phenomenon, which has been driving wars all over the world. He rejects the notion of permanent ""ancient hatreds" as an explanation and finds the roots of ethnic violence in myths and symbols, the stories groups tell about who they are. Ethnic wars result from the politics of these myths and symbols, mobilized not so much to address political interests as to stir emotions and political loyalties.

metaphor,[20] and indeed also a mirror[21] for much of postcolonial Africa. But it is this observation that makes the question of the difference that Christianity and the church makes in the context of political violence in postcolonial Africa even more pressing.

New Directions in Missiological Reflection

If the question of the Christian difference in the context of political violence became heightened for me in the wake of the Rwanda genocide, what also increasingly became clear is that for theological and missiological reflection to investigate and display the Christian difference in the context of Africa's ethnic struggles, it would have to assume a new starting point—a starting point that does not assume ethnic or cultural identity as the unquestionable point of reference for mission. Such reflection would have to constantly point to stories and models within which exemplary interruptions of violence could be made evident. At the same time, such reflection would not only seek to account for the logic that makes such interruptions possible but would also seek to narrate these interruptions as instantiations of an anthropology that reconfigures ethnicity within a distinctive Christian telos.

Lessons from Rwanda: Christian Mission as the Formation of a Community That Supersedes Ethnic Tags

When I first began thinking about this missiological task, I did not know where to turn for an example of the kind of anthropology that could reconfigure ethnicity within a distinctive Christian telos. However, as I reflected more on the genocide, I found myself drawn to the stories of communities and individuals who did not participate in the killing and who thus provide rather fresh resources for thinking about Christian mission in the face of political violence. The case of the Muslim community is particularly telling. In contrast to the accounts of the mass participation of Christians in the genocide, there are many testimonies to the protection that members of the Muslim community gave each other, and that

---

[20]Mamdani, *When Victims Become Killers*, ix.

[21]See my *Mirror to the Church: Resurrecting Faith after Genocide in Rwanda* (Grand Rapids, MI: Zondervan, 2009).

Muslims refused to divide themselves ethnically.[22] In reflecting on this fact, Gérard Prunier gives as a possible reason the strong sense of solidarity among Muslims that goes beyond ethnicity:

> This solidarity comes from the fact that "being Muslim" in Rwanda, where Muslims are a very small (0.2 percent) proportion of the population, is not simply a choice dictated by religion: it is a global identity choice. Muslims are often marginal people and this reinforces a strong sense of community identification which supersedes ethnic tags, something the majority Christians have not been able to achieve.[23]

I found this explanation by Prunier quite insightful and also quite provocative. For in the context of a social history where "ethnicity" has become a regular feature of political violence in Africa, the formation of communities whose sense of solidarity "supersedes ethnic tags" is what Christian mission should aim for.

Another story that arrested my attention was that of a Hutu boy with a "confused" identity. He fled to the bush during the genocide. After two or three weeks, the Tutsis pointed out to him that he was Hutu and so could be saved. He left the marshes and was not attacked. But the boy had spent so much time with Tutsis in his early childhood that he was now confused about ethnic groups and did not know how to draw the "proper" line between them. Afterwards, when he returned to the village, he did not get involved in the killing. The *Intarahamwe* did not force him to kill because he was, in their words, "clearly overwhelmed."[24]

That this boy was confused about his identity is illuminating, for in his "confusion" he embodied the kind of "anthropological naiveté"[25] that points to the possibility of an identity and a com-

---

[22]See, e.g., Gérard Prunier, *The Rwanda Crisis: History of a Genocide* (New York: Columbia University Press, 1997).

[23]Ibid., 253.

[24]Jean Hatzfeld, *Machete Season: The Killers in Rwanda Speak* (New York: Farrar, Straus and Giroux, 2003), 122–23.

[25]On the notion of "anthropological naiveté," see my *Mirror to the Church*, 71. It was in view of this anthropological naiveté that mission both assumes and engenders that led me to the conclusion that "the goal of mission is the formation of a new people in the world. The church's primary purpose is not to make America more Christian, but make American Christians less American and Rwanda

munity that "supersedes ethnic tags." And just like the Muslim community, the confused boy provided a fresh interruption and an alternative to the madness of ethnicity during the genocide. But what theological and missiological frameworks could account for such examples, not as odd and exceptional occurrences within Christian history, but as the exemplary illumination of the gift of Christian mission in Africa? The work of the missiologist Andrew Walls provides one such answer.

Andrew Walls on the Pilgrim Principle and Ephesian Moments

In "The Gospel as Prisoner and Liberator of Culture,"[26] Andrew Walls notes that church history has always been a battleground for two opposing tendencies—each of which has its origin in the Gospel: the indigenizing and pilgrim principles, respectively. Whereas the indigenizing principle means that one cannot totally separate from one's culture, the pilgrim principle points to the Gospel as a dynamic process that takes one out of one's culture.

> On the one hand, it is of the essence of the Gospel that God accepts us as we are, on the ground of Christ's work alone, not on the ground of what we have become or are trying to become. But, if He accepts us "as we are" that implies he does not take us as isolated, self-governing units, because we are not. We are conditioned by a particular time and place, by our family and group and society, by "culture" in fact. In Christ God accepts us together with our group relations, with that cultural conditioning that makes us feel at home in one part of human society and less at home in another.[27]

Although this is true, Walls goes on to state,

> Throughout Church history there has been another force in tension with this indigenizing principle, and this also is

---

Christians less Rwandan" (ibid., 156).

[26]See Andrew Walls, *The Missionary Movement in Christian History: Studies in the Transmission of Faith* (Maryknoll, NY: Orbis Books, 2004).

[27]Ibid., 7.

equally true of the Gospel. Not only does God in Christ take people as they are: He takes them in order to transform them into what He wants them to be. Along with the indigenizing principle which makes his faith a place to feel at home, the Christian inherits the pilgrim principle, which whispers to him that he has no abiding city and warns him that to be faithful to Christ will put him out of step with his society; for that society never existed, in East or West, ancient time or modern, which would absorb the word of Christ painlessly into its system.[28]

The fact of these two principles leads to a creative tension within the life of the Christian and within world Christianity. For while the indigenizing principle means that to live as a Christian is to live as a member of a particular society, community, tribe, and nation, the pilgrim principle points to the constant identity crisis that mission creates as it invites us, in the words of Charles Willie, "to live in, between, and beyond the boundaries of [our] race, culture, tribe or nation."[29] This of course has far-reaching political implications, which Walls does not explore in his essay, although he does note that because of the pilgrim principle, God takes people out of their particular culture "in order to transform them into what He wants them to be."[30] However, if we read this

---

[28]Ibid., 8.

[29]Willie calls this "in-between" the space of marginal creativity, which gives those at the margins fresh possibilities for understanding and engaging reality. See Charles V. Willie, *Theories of Human Social Action* (Dix Hills, NY: General Hall, 1994), 99, quoted in Curtis de Young, *Living Faith: How Faith Inspires Social Justice* (Minneapolis: Fortress Press, 2007), 53.

[30]Walls's aim in drawing attention to these two principles is to press for cultural openness on behalf of Western Christians in the face of the shifting center of gravity to the Global South. Such a shift will inevitably generate new theologies that reflect the concerns and aspirations of the Christians and communities in the Global South. Since every theology (thanks to the indigenizing principle) is culturally bound, these theologies will no doubt sound odd to the ears of Western Christians (just as much of Western theology sounds odd to the ears of African Christians). But since no theologies are self-sufficient, the rise of new theologies will not only contribute to the rich diversity within Christianity, it is also an opportunity for the development of a fuller meaning of the Gospel, which lies beyond any one particular culture. Given this primary interest, the political import of the two principles, particularly the pilgrim principle, remains unexplored in this essay.

essay in connection with another by Walls, "The Ephesian Moment," then the political import of Christian mission becomes explicit, for it is evident that the reason that God takes people outside their culture is for God to create a new people in the world.[31] This new people, whose community identification supersedes all ethnic tags, was historically reflected in the community of Ephesus, where Jewish and Gentile Christians came together in a rather remarkable "Ephesian Moment."[32]

Walls notes that it is this coming together of two communities historically separated—the breaking down of the wall of separation brought about by Christ's death (Eph 2:13–18)—that Paul celebrates in the letter to the Ephesians. Jewish and Gentile Christians are "no longer strangers and sojourners, but fellow citizens" and "members of God's household" (2:19). Thus if the letter to the Ephesians recognizes the cultural and political realities of being Jew and Gentile, this is not what Paul celebrates, but the fact of their "coming together": of their being "made alive together" (2:5), "raised up together, and sitting together" (2:6). Jewish and Gentile Christians "belong together" as "bricks—used in the construction of a single building—the temple where the One God would live" (2:19–22). They do not constitute two separate communities, but one community, of which they are both members, constituting as it were different parts of a single body of which "Christ is the head, the mind, the brain, under whose control the whole body works and is held together" (4:15–16).

A number of things become clear from Paul's letter to the Ephesians. First, it is the "coming *together*" (which Paul expresses variously as being "made alive *together*," "raised up *together*," "sitting *together*") of the different cultural elements that reveals the "very height of Christ's full stature." As Walls states:

> The very height of Christ's full stature is reached only by the coming together of the different cultural entities into the body of Christ. They belong together as one of them is

---

[31]Andrew F. Walls, "The Ephesian Moment: At a Crossroads in Christian History," in Andrew F. Walls, *The Cross-Cultural Process in Christian History* (Maryknoll, NY: Orbis Books, 2002).

[32]The reflections in the following section draw heavily from my essay "Mission and the Ephesian Moment of World Christianity."

incomplete without the other. Only "together," not on our own, can we reach his full stature."[33]

Second, what the description points to is that the coming together of different cultural elements creates something new: a new people and a new community in the world.

Third, as Walls notes, the expression and test of that coming together was the meal table: "Two cultures historically separated by the meal table were not able to come together at table to share the knowledge of Christ."[34] Thus, the meal table—the institution that had once symbolized the ethnic and cultural division—now became the hallmark of Christian living. The expression of this new identity and community is not something *spiritual* (in the sense of wafting above the mundane and material), but a very concrete and tangible community that emerges, takes shape, and gets reaffirmed in the concrete practices of sharing life together. The story of the seminary community at Buta provides a good illumination of such an Ephesian community, and so by telling their story we might get a better sense of gift of the Gospel in shaping a culture of peace in Africa, but also of the concrete practices through which that gift of peace is nurtured.

The Witness of Buta

The attack on Buta has to be located within the broader story of political violence in Burundi, within which "ethnicity" was reinforced and reproduced as an unquestioned building block of Burundian society. A German colony until 1919, Burundi came under Belgian rule, which, using the same Hamitic mythology as in Rwanda, divided the country neatly along Hutu, Tutsi, and Twa identities, affirmed (as natural allies) Tutsi privilege while setting up a system of political and economic administration that marginalized the majority Hutu. Unlike Rwanda to the North, Burundi's independence in 1962 left the Tutsi in power, but the "ethnic" hatred between the groups set the framework for Burundi's post-independence history, which has been marked by

---

[33]Ibid.
[34]Walls, "Ephesian Moment," 78.

political instability, a series of coups d'état, and massacres that have pitted Hutus and Tutsis in an endless cycle of revenge and counterrevenge. The fact that Burundi's 10 million people speak the same language and that more than 80 percent are Christian, with Catholicism as the dominant religion, seems not to make much difference.

Following the assassination of President Melchior Ndadaye (the first Hutu president), in 1993, the Hutus began to wreak revenge by killing Tutsi neighbors. A devastating civil war ensued as extremists on both sides carried out massacres throughout the country. A number of schools closed. In fact, by 1997 as "ethnic" tension mounted, Buta was not only one the few schools that remained open, it was the only one where students from both ethnicities lived together and continued to study as normally as possible. This was in great part due to the leadership of the rector, Father Zacharie Bukuru, who both encouraged the students to remain at school and, through a number of programs, formed the students into a rare community whose sense of solidarity superseded ethnic tags.

The first of these programs involved a rereading of Burundi's history. In his account of the events that led to the attack on Buta,[35] Father Bukuru notes that in the wake of the assassination of the president, he was deeply saddened

> by how quickly my students, who had previously gotten along well together, came to consider one another as strangers and even enemies, each ethnicity accusing the other of being congenital assassins. I heard all the standard ethnic prejudices on their lips: "they're all like that—they're bloodthirsty savages—we've already been told that this is what it was like in 1972 . . ." etc. (32)

It was this realization that led Father Bukuru to undertake "the difficult yet necessary rereading of our history" (32). Thus every evening after dinner he would gather students for an hour for a

---

[35]Zacharie Bukuru, *Les quarante jeunes martyrs de Buta (Burundi 1997): Frères à la vie, à la mort* (Paris: Karthala, 2004). The page numbers (in text within parentheses) refer to the unpublished English translation by Jodi Mikalachki—*The Forty Martyrs of Burundi*.

"rector's talk," and used this time to retell the history of Burundi, showing how there were no clear victims and perpetrators, but that both Tutsi and Hutu were at once victims and perpetrators. Moreover, he led the students to see that the real effect of the "ethnic" factor in Burundi's history and politics was to prevent Burundians from seeing the real problems of the country. For in fact the majority of Burundians (Tutsi and Hutu alike) were impoverished, and it made little difference whether the president was Hutu or Tutsi, from the North or the South.

Second, Father Bukuru led "a merciless war on lies and rumors" that were the source of much fear and anxiety in the student community (34). One way he did this was to devote the second part of the nightly meetings to dialogue—as an open forum for students to ask questions and voice their fears and anxieties. During this dialogue time, the students were encouraged to retell the rumors they had heard, and these were then openly discussed. Shy students were encouraged to write their comments or questions down ahead of time to make sure no students were excluded. The dialogues also provided an opportunity for students to name the prejudices against each ethnic group as a way to take the sting out of the "verbal violence" (33) of the ethnic prejudices. In order for the forums not to turn into personal attacks, clear rules of order had to be established: if a student spoke insultingly of another, he would be required to leave the room for a few minutes, and when he returned he would have to apologize to the whole group. Since the rector loved all the students, without discriminating between Hutu and Tutsi, and constantly referred to them as "my children," he was able to treat them evenhandedly: "My love for them allowed me to be strict when necessary, without fear of being judged" (34).

The overall effect of these nightly forums was a culture of truth, truth-telling, and trust that began to form within the student community. As the evening meetings and forums went on, the students "debated all political issues, taking care to name them and to seek their origins without trying to hide anything" (35). As a result, "there was no need to dream of taking up arms like other youth in the country in order to find justice. This dialogue gave us relief. It healed us" (35).

Communal work and recreation exercises also helped to forge a spirit of unity and relaxation. Father Bukuru notes:

We welcomed everything that might promote laughter and relaxation between the two ethnic groups: sporting competitions, matches between classes, between students and teachers, between seniors and juniors, cross country races, manual labor that offered the chance to sing together, games, theater, dance, lectures, and festive meals shared by teachers and students. All these things changed the face of the seminary. (37)

Dance played a particularly significant role in healing, but also in cementing the unity between ethnic groups. For example, the Kirundi traditional dance (which both ethnic groups shared and enjoyed), "called us beyond ourselves into generosity, joy, relaxation, sharing, dialogue, and purity" and "brought us together in a single culture, uniting us in something beyond our differences in ethnicity, age, or social status" (38). In fact, dance became another form of prayer, and so on weekends the seminary "alternated modern dance, traditional dance and song, and night prayers" (38).

Through these and many other shared activities, the boys were so filled with a spirit of fraternity that they began to create their own clubs and associations, including a local chapter of Music for Hope International.[36] They also founded an AIDS awareness organization and an environment club, through which they organized lectures at the seminary and performed outreach in the surrounding local communities. Through these and other activities the reputation of Buta as a unique and rare example of solidarity that went beyond ethnicity spread in the country. And while this reputation earned them admiration (the prime minister visited the school and donated a female calf), it also earned them a number of enemies, from either side of the ethnic divide, who regarded them as "traitors." It is perhaps not surprising, therefore, that among those who attacked the school were three former students who had left the school because they had found the idea of unity not only impossible but "dangerous."

---

[36]Inspired by the Argentinean pianist Miguel Angel Estrella, one of the objectives of the Musique Espérance is to promote equal opportunities and access to a culture of peace, mostly for children and teenagers, through music programs that can raise active participation and solidarity awareness. See http://federation-musique-esperance.org.

On Winning the War on Political Violence

The story of Buta offers a number of key lessons in thinking about Christianity and the prospects for peace in the context of political violence in Africa. First, building a community whose solidarity exceeds ethnic tags should not be seen as an *extra* dimension but as an *essential* dimension of the preaching of the Gospel. In telling the story of how a culture of solidarity took shape at Buta, Father Bukuru notes how the central role of prayer, worship, and other spiritual activities (retreats, devotions, etc.) served as both the glue and the spring that "replenished our strength to live together in unity." What this essential spiritual dimension means is that unity is "more a grace from God than the fruit of our own efforts." In the end, he notes, the unity was realized effortlessly not as an external political idea, but as a constituent and internal reality of the life of the Christian: "The unconditional acceptance of the other is at the heart of the Gospel" (39).

Second, I have narrated these activities in order to highlight the work, effort, and time that is required to build an Ephesian community marked by trust and solidarity among ethnic groups. In the case of Buta it took the determined effort of the rector and his staff to build the necessary practices and disciplines into the daily rhythm and way of life of the community.

Third, within the social history of Burundi, characterized by ethnic rivalry and violence, Buta provides a much needed fresh interruption and alternative and confirms the possibility of another way of living together, another history, another anthropology, and another politics. But this is also what makes an Ephesian community like Buta "dangerous": it threatens the vested interests of the politics of ethnicity. The deaths of the forty young students and the injury of many more because they refused to separate into ethnic groups confirms the courage required to live in the political imagination of the Ephesian moment. But their martyrdom also confirms that the existence of Ephesian communities like Buta does not promise to make the world safer since there are those who will always be willing to kill to advance a politics based on lies and violence.

And yet, finally, without the story and witness of communities like Buta, "the full height of Christ's full stature" remains simply an idea, a theory, not a concrete political reality. For it is communities like Buta that both reveal and confirm the truth of the Gospel, namely that Christ has broken down the wall of separation and that we are "no longer strangers and sojourners, but fellow citizens" and "members of God's household" (Eph 2:19). This is the victory that the dying boy so simply but so eloquently put into words: "Father, we have won. They told us to separate and we refused. We have won." In the context of Africa's ongoing cycles of political violence we need many more such examples and accounts of winning.

7

"Threatened with Resurrection"

The Terrible Gift of Martyrs

It is something within us
that doesn't let us sleep,
that doesn't let us rest,
that won't stop pounding
deep inside . . . .
What keeps us from sleeping
is that they have threatened us with Resurrection!
—Julia Esquivel, *Threatened with Resurrection*

We live in a world marked by war, poverty, injustice, and all sorts of destructive conflicts. Ours is also a world in which the social programs we have to address these problems seem ineffective, or in some cases even end up exposing deeper social divisions. It is therefore not surprising that in the face of what seem to be intractable challenges, there is a growing sense of despair and cynicism about goodness and peace in the world. Many try to mask this cynicism by adopting a posture of pragmatic realism: the world is the way it is. Nothing much can be done about it. All one has to do is to maximize any good or opportunities there are in the world for one's own survival or for the well-being of

This essay originally appeared as "Threatened with Resurrection: Martyrdom and Reconciliation in the World Church," in *Witness of the Body: The Past, Present and Future of Christian Martyrdom*, ed. Michael L Budde (Grand Rapids, MI: Eerdmans, 2011), 190–203. Reproduced here with permission of the publisher.

one's loved ones. But this pragmatic individualism is itself another form of hopelessness.

What is needed, if we are to avoid this type of hopelessness, are not simply more strategies and skills that purport to "fix" the brokenness of the world (important as these might be), but stories worth living for (and therefore dying for) in the midst of the world's brokenness. It is such a story that Paul points to in 2 Corinthians 5:17:

> So, whoever is in Christ, there is a new creation. The old world has passed away. The new is here. All this is from God, who has reconciled us to himself through Christ and given the ministry of reconciliation.

For Paul the hope of the story, which reconciliation names, is not a static state of peace, whatever that might mean, but an invitation to a journey. Moreover, as is clear from the passage in Corinthians just cited, the invitation to this journey is not limited to a few individuals; it is to all who have been baptized ("whoever is in Christ") In fact, elsewhere Paul shows that the journey is not limited only to Christians, but that all human beings, indeed the whole of God's creation, is on this journey and "awaits with eager longing" the freedom of God's new creation (Rom 8:19–23).

In this essay I would like to show that Christian martyrs, in their lives and deaths, provide the most concrete, dynamic, and exemplary case of the journey of reconciliation. Specifically, I would like to show that the journey that the martyrs exemplify provides the church and the world with a dangerous hope in that it is a hope that both invites and threatens the church into a life of vigil, a life of social struggle, and a new and resurrected community. Without these gifts, Christians would not know what it means to live as a people of hope in a broken and violent world.

Martyrdom: A Dangerous Hope

In naming martyrs the church declares men and women who have lived in an exemplary way and have paid the ultimate sacrifice as *living* witnesses—that is, as witnesses who, although dead, are still with us. One must be careful not to romanticize the martyrs still "being with us." Their presence with us is a fact to be at once celebrated and feared. For, on the one hand, to the extent that they are with us still, they are "our friends"—part of the cloud of witnesses (Heb 11) who inspire, support, encourage, and journey with us. On the other hand, their being in our midst also *threatens* us with resurrection and constantly keeps us from sleeping.

Those familiar with the life of the Guatemalan dissident Julia Esquivel might immediately recognize that I am drawing from her poem *Threatened with Resurrection*. Since her poem provides a helpful way of exploring the odd presence that martyrs are in our midst, and thus the dangerous hope they exemplify, it might be helpful to quote her at length.

A schoolteacher forced into exile from her native Guatemala, Julia Esquivel writes:

> It is something within us that doesn't let us sleep,
> that doesn't let us rest,
> that won't stop pounding
> deep inside,
> it is the silent, warm weeping
> of Indian women without their husbands,
> it is the sad gaze of the children
> fixed somewhere beyond memory,
> precious in our eyes
> which during sleep,
> though closed, keep watch
> systole,
> diastole,
> awake.
> Now six have left us,
> and nine in Rabinal,
> and two, plus two, plus two,
> and ten, a hundred, a thousand,
> a whole army
> witness to our pain,
> our fear,
> our courage,
> our *hope*!

What keeps us from sleeping
is that they have threatened us with Resurrection![1]

As Parker Palmer[2] rightly notes from the poem, it is not immediately clear who it is that "threatens us with resurrection." On the one hand, Esquivel seems to be speaking of the killers—those who have killed hundreds of peasants in Rabinal, who threaten those still alive. On the other hand, however, it seems the threat of resurrection comes not from the killers but from the dead themselves. In the end, as Parker Palmer suggests, "the poem imitates life, in which the 'threat of resurrection' comes both from those who dispense death and from those who have died in the hope of new life."[3]

The implications for this observation are significant:

If it is true that both killers and the killed threaten us with resurrection, then we are caught between a rock and a hard place. On the one hand, we fear the killers, but not simply because they want to kill us. We fear them because they test our convictions about resurrection; they test our willingness to be brought into a larger life than the one we now know. On the other hand, we fear the innocent victims of the killers, those who have died for love and justice and peace. Though they are our friends, we fear them because they call us to follow them in the "marathon of Hope." If we were to take their calling seriously, we ourselves would have to undergo some form of dying.[4]

Palmer continues:

Caught between the killers and the killed, we . . . huddle together in a conspiracy of silence, trying to ignore the ambiguous call of the new life that lies beyond death. Julia

---

[1] Julia Esquivel, *Threatened with Resurrection*, 2nd ed. (Elgin, IL: Brethren Press, 1994), 59–61.

[2] Parker Palmer, *The Active Life* (San Francisco: Jossey-Bass, 1990), 139–57.

[3] Ibid., 147.

[4] Ibid., 148.

Esquivel is trying to break up our little huddle, I think, trying to inspire our active lives, calling us to engage the demented gorillas as well as our martyred friends, calling us to walk into our fear of resurrection and to open ourselves to the life on the other side.[5]

I find Parker's observations about Esquivel's poem particularly helpful in understanding the dangerous hope exemplified by the martyrs. The odd gift that martyrs are to the church and to the world lies precisely in their ability to break our little huddles of fear. In doing so, they keep the church from sleeping as the constant "pounding" of their memory energizes the church into a life of struggle and invites Christians into a new communion—a resurrected community on the other side of death. That is why the church can offer no more determinative sign of hope than to name and celebrate the memory of martyrs. For in so doing the church draws attention to at least three critical gifts: vigilance, social struggle, and dreaming. Without these gifts the journey of reconciliation cannot be sustained. In the following three sections, I briefly explore these gifts as the hallmark of what it means to be a sign of hope and an agent of God's new creation in a broken world.

A Life of Vigilance: The Politics of Naming

> That is the whirlwind
> which does not let us sleep,
> the reason why sleeping, we keep watch,
> and awake, we dream.
> —Julia Esquivel, *Threatened with Resurrection*

Martyrs keep the church from sleeping. In many places in *Threatened with Resurrection*, Esquivel speaks of being kept from sleeping. What Esquivel is obviously referring to is not the lack of sleep otherwise known as insomnia, but a form of watchfulness. That is the reason she notes, "why sleeping, we keep watch." It is through such a vigil that one can keep an eye on those who sacrifice the innocent.

---

[5]Ibid.

Apparently, the early Christians knew something of this watchfulness, for they had no illusion that the world in which they lived was hospitable to the Christian way of life. That is one reason why Christian feast days and holy days were marked by a "vigil" service. This was not simply a way of anticipating the celebration of the feast day with prayer and other liturgical commemoration. It was a reminder of the vigilance that, even in the midst of celebration, Christian life was all about. But this is also the same reason why, as Pope John Paul II reminds us, despite considerable organizational difficulties, the church of the first centuries took care to write down in special martyrologies the witness of the martyrs.[6] The reason, it is now obvious, is that the cultivation of a life of vigil requires and involves memory. Keeping the memory of martyrs was at least one way of remembering the gift (journey) that the Christian life was all about, as well as naming particular dangers, threats, and temptations on the journey.

In our time, we have greatly lost the sense of the world as a dangerous place. This may sound ironic given the ever-present reality of war, injustice, and conflict. What we have lost is the ability to see these challenges as specifically *Christian* challenges (and not simply as human challenges). Furthermore, we have little sense of the Christian life as a journey, according to which we live in the world as "resident aliens."[7] As a result, we have come to be so much at home in the world that we readily accept explanations that purport to offer the ultimate account of reality. Thus, sociological accounts lead us to think that conflict and war are inevitable; we accept the fact of millions of people going without food as simply an unfortunate consequence of the economic realities of our world. We easily assume "race," "tribe," and "nationality" as natural identities.

How else does one explain Rwanda 1994: that the majority Hutu Christians tried to wipe out their Tutsi brothers and sisters in the 1994 genocide? The fact that they were all Christians and this happened to be Easter season did not seem to register any

---

[6]John Paul II, Apostolic Letter, *Tertio Millennio Adveniente* (Rome, 1994), no. 37.

[7]For a full discussion of Christians as "resident aliens" see Stanley Hauerwas and Will Willimon, *Resident Aliens: Life in the Christian Colony* (Nashville, TN: Abingdon, 1989).

significant difference. In order to pierce through the tragic horror of such tribalism,[8] but also to call the church back to a life of vigil—a life of alertness and resistance—one needs the story of martyrs like Chantal Mujjawamaholo and her friends.

On March 18, 1997, three years after the genocide, Interahamwe militia attacked the secondary school at Nyange in Rwanda. The students had finished supper and their evening prayer and were in the classrooms doing their prep. The rebels attacked Senior 4 and Senior 5 classes and asked the students to separate Tutsi and Hutu. The students refused, saying they were all Rwandans. The rebels shot at them indiscriminately and threw grenades in the classroom. Thirteen students were killed. The victims were all reclaimed by their families and buried at their homes, except one girl, who was from Changugu (a long distance away). She is buried at school. Her tombstone bears the simple inscription: Chantal Mujjawamaholo. B.24.04.1975. D. 18.03.1997. She was just a month shy of her twenty-second birthday when she was killed.[9]

In a world marked by tribal, racial, and national identities, where we tend to assume these identities as natural, we need the story of Chantal and her friends to confirm the idolatrous nature of these so-called natural identities. In this case, the truth that Mujjawamaholo and her martyred friends depict by their refusing to divide between Hutu and Tutsi points to resistance as a necessary posture in the face of these identities. But even more important, their story points to the gift, for the sake of which resistance is possible and necessary. Thus martyrs name the telos of Christian life. Without a clear sense of the gift toward which one's life is directed, resistance can be a form of reckless self-sacrifice or merely an expression of radical fundamentalism.[10]

---

[8] I have argued elsewhere that the depth and type of tribalism revealed in the Rwanda genocide is not an exclusively African but a widespread and constant and consistent pattern within modern nation-state formation. See Katongole, "Christianity, Tribalism, and the Rwandan Genocide," *Logos: A Journal of Catholic Thought and Culture* 8, no. 3 (2005): 67–93.

[9] Notes from author's visit to the school. December 21, 2004.

[10] This marks the difference between a life of martyrdom Christianly understood and terrorism that may involve suicide. Martyrs do not want to die; and even if they are willing to sacrifice their own lives for the gift, they believe that the gift is not in their own power to realize. Accordingly, they can never sacrifice others in order to bring about the peace for which they are willing to die. In fact, their

That is why martyrs name the gift. The students' refusal to separate Hutu and Tutsi, saying they were all Rwandans, names not only a sense of solidarity but also a friendship that cuts across, and whose promise is far richer than, the ideological promises of Hutu or Tutsi. But even more tellingly, Chantal's very name of *Mujjawamaholo*, which in Kinyarwanda means "maiden of peace," points to the gift and goal of Christian living, whose truth and reality can be grasped only to the extent that one is able to resist the many forms of tribalism that characterize our existence in the world.

I am therefore not simply suggesting that the church should name Chantal Mujjawamaholo and her friends as martyrs; I am making the stronger claim that martyrs name the church for what she is—maiden of peace. Without the story of Chantal and her friends, this invitation, call, and gift can very easily be obscured in the assumed inevitability of racial, tribal, or national politics. Martyrs provide a constant reminder of both the Christian gift as well as the concrete challenges to living out that invitation and journey.

This is the reason why the practice of choosing a baptismal name (often the name of a martyr or saint) has deep significance in the Catholic tradition to the extent that these names serve as geographies of memory, which keep the church from forgetting—or from sleeping, to use Esquivel's metaphor. This ancient practice resonates well with many African traditions, where naming is always a rich cultural event. The naming of a baby is never a private or family matter; it is a social event, and the name is understood not simply as personal tag, chosen because it is "cute," but as the embodiment of social memory and a form of practical wisdom.

That is what makes the story of Blessed Annuarite Nengapeta (beatified by Pope John Paul II in 1985) from the Congo so remarkable. As a young girl, Annuarite joined the convent of the Holy Family Sisters in Isiro-Wamba, where she spent her religious life as a nun and a midwife. In 1964, when the Mulele rebellion broke out, Simba rebels invaded the convent. Annuarite was

---

willingness to die is a confirmation of their belief that such peace has already been given by the one whose death and resurrection we remember. All we are called upon to be as Christians is to witness that peace, which might involve surrendering our own lives—a strange kind of peace indeed.

murdered as she resisted the sexual demands of the rebel leader.

Annuarite's encouragement to her other sisters during the siege as well as her courage during the ordeal is exemplary. The witness of her names is also striking. At birth, she received the name of Nengapeta, which in her native language means, "wealth is deceptive." When she started primary school she was registered by error with the name Annuarite. That was the name of her sister. In her language the name meant, "I laugh to myself about war."

That is why in naming martyrs the church not only names her own identity as a maiden of peace. In the life and name of someone like Annuarite Nengapeta, the church also learns to rightly name the spells[11] that try to convince us that conflict, war, and violence are inevitable, or that the world as we know it is the only world we have to live in. Only if we are able to name the spells for what they are, are we able to cultivate the virtue of alertness through which we are able to resist, despise, or laugh at the ideologies that would willingly sacrifice lives in the name of "peace," wealth, democracy, development, and security.

A Life of Struggle: Gestures of Peaceableness

> They have threatened us with resurrection,
> because they are more alive than ever before,
> because they transform our agonies,
> and fertilize our struggle.
> —Julia Esquivel, *Threatened with Resurrection*

There are at least two ways in which martyrs keep the church from sleeping by calling it into a life of commitment to realize a better world. First, martyrs fertilize the church's struggle by drawing the church into a restless posture of lament.

Even though martyrs can be said to be dead, and thus resting in God, they are never really dead; and they never really rest, since they remain, even in death, restless. According to the vision in the book of Revelation, the souls of those below the altar remain restless.

---

[11]For the language of "spells" as it applies to modern ideologies, see Emmanuel Katongole, "Violence and Christian Social Reconstruction in Africa," *Other Journal* (August 2005), http://www.theotherjournal.com.

> When he [the angel] broke open the fifth seal, I saw underneath the altar, the souls of those who had been slaughtered for the word of God and for the testimony they had given; they cried out with a loud voice, "Sovereign Lord, holy and true, how long will it be before you judge and avenge our blood on the inhabitants of the earth?" (Rev 6:9–10)

If this is the fate of martyrs, then a church that is the custodian of their stories finds itself inevitably drawn into the same restless cry of "how long?" Such a cry is at once a posture of lament, which allows Christians to see the extent and depth of brokenness, and a posture of defiance, as it brings the church to the same anger and 'breaking point'[12]—a point where "we cannot take it anymore."

The recovery of such anger and passion is a much-needed gift, especially in our time when most of the church's ministry is carried out as if nothing much is really at stake (save perhaps the church's own institutional security, or the spiritual security of her members). The restless cry of the martyrs keeps the church from sleeping by reminding it of the promise of new creation for which the martyrs laid down their lives.

That is why the lament of "how long, O God" that the martyrs evoke is not a forlorn cry of despair but a form of hope that galvanizes the church into a passionate and relentless struggle for a better society, where human life and dignity are respected, basic human needs are met, and peace and freedom abound. The cry of the martyrs calls us to a place where hope becomes concrete in forgiveness, respect, and tolerance.

Second, the martyrs call us back into the everydayness of the struggle for peace. Even though the martyrs are honored for the ultimate sacrifice of their lives, it is not primarily their deaths but the very mundane gestures and practice of peaceableness in their everyday living that are the point. That is why it is not the memory of the martyrs in abstract that is important, but the telling and retelling of the thick narrative of their particular lives.

When I visited Nyange Secondary School in December 2004

---

[12]Brian K. Blount, "Breaking Point: A Sermon," in *Lament: Reclaiming Practices in Pulpit, Pew, and Public Square*, ed. Sally A. Brown and Patrick D. Miller (Louisville, KY: Westminster John Knox, 2005), 145–53.

and heard the story of Chantal Mujjawamaholo and her friends, I inquired after the possible explanations why the students were willing to risk their lives rather than divide into two groups: Hutu and Tutsi. Where did such courage come from? A teacher at the school noted that the students had just finished their evening prayers and so could have drawn spiritual strength from that. But he also spoke about another teacher, who had since left the school, who had taught a course in unity and nonviolence. Every morning before the classes, this teacher would speak to the students and give them some insights into unity and nonviolence.

These practices of evening prayers and classes about unity and nonviolence show that in a world that is so enamored of grand strategies for how to end poverty and eradicate terrorism, the martyrs remind us that the journey of reconciliation is a journey of tactics and gestures—a story here, a lesson there, some insights.

In this world of gestures, tactics, and ordinary practices the martyrs show us the stuff of God's new creation as well as the form and the location of the struggle to realize a different world.

A Life of Dreaming: A Communion of Witnesses

> To dream awake,
> to keep watch asleep,
> to live while dying
> and to know ourselves already
> resurrected!
> —Julia Esquivel, *Threatened with Resurrection*

If the martyrs fertilize the church's struggle for a better, more peaceful world, what sustains that struggle is the gift of dreaming. Although a life of dreaming might strike some as a fantasy (as in "daydreaming"), the type of dreaming that the martyrs call the church into is a very concrete discipline. It is a way of living into the future as if the future were already here. Another way to put it is to say that the vision of God's peaceful creation is not a fantastic dream, one that can only be realized in the afterlife, but a concrete possibility in the here and now. That is why to dream, at least in the sense I am using it here, is at the same time to open ourselves to the life on the other side of death; it is to live a life of the resurrection, or in the words of Esquivel's poem, it is to know oneself already resurrected.

No doubt opening oneself to life on the other side of death not only requires courage but also a certain amount of madness—the sort of madness that Thomas Sankara, the Burkina Faso revolutionary who was slain in 1987, had in mind when he noted:

> You cannot carry out fundamental change without a certain amount of madness. In this case, it comes from non-conformity; the ability to turn your back on old formulas; the courage to invent the future. . . . We must dare to invent the future.[13]

This is the same type of madness—of daring to invent the future—that the martyrs threaten the church with. And that is what makes resurrection both a gift and a threat. In a world built on assumptions of power, self-preservation, and control, the martyrs reveal to us a new future that is built on powerlessness. For, in their being killed, the martyrs are indeed powerless. In their powerlessness, they seem to have nothing to lose. Accordingly, they stand naked in front of their killers and face death.

But if the martyrs seem to have nothing to lose, it is because, as Esquivel says, they know themselves already resurrected. In this way, what they reveal and live into is a vision of the future made present, a radical sense of flourishing that cannot be threatened, not even by death.[14]

But if the life of resurrection is a threat, it is also as Esquivel says, a *marvelous* adventure:

---

[13] Thomas Sankara, *Thomas Sankara Speaks: The Burkina Faso Revolution 1983–87*, trans. Samantha Anderson (New York: Pathfinder, 1988), 144.

[14] That is why, in light of the above considerations, and given the courage and hope martyrs exemplify, the crucial question for the Christian is not whether to live or die, but how to die better, which is to say, how to live and die without fear. A book that speaks directly to the issue of fear is Scott Bader-Saye, *Following Jesus in a Culture of Fear* (Grand Rapids, MI: Brazos, 2007). Another inspiring story is that of Robert Sobukwe, an early resister of apartheid in South Africa, who was—imprisoned on Robben Island and banished into solitary confinement—but who nevertheless remained hopeful and committed to the struggle. His biography is appropriately titled *How Can Man Die Better?* See Benjamin Pogrund, *How Can Man Die Better: Sobukwe and Apartheid* (London: Peter Halban, 1990).

> Join us in this vigil
> and you will know what it is to dream!
> Then you will know how marvelous it is
> to live threatened with Resurrection![15]

What makes it marvelous is the fact that a life of dreaming both requires and creates a community. And so even though martyrs may seem to die alone, what makes it possible for them to willingly accept death is the fact that they are never alone, but that the story and struggle they participate in is bigger than them; it is a story into which they have been called, but one that will continue after them. In the words of Esquivel again:

> because in this marathon of Hope,
> there are always others to relieve us
> who carry the strength
> to reach the finish line
> which lies beyond death.[16]

This observation is significant because in a world so marked by individualism, the story of martyrs points to and names the church as a body of witnesses. Moreover, in a world marked by the deep divisions of racial, national, and ethnic loyalties, what martyrs name is a communion that cuts across these boundaries. This is what the story of Tonia Locatelli reveals.

Following the RPF (Rwanda Patriotic Front) invasion of Rwanda in 1990 local militias together with the police started a systematic process of killing Tutsis at Nyamata. In 1992, an Italian social worker, Tonia Locatelli, who had lived in Rwanda for over twenty years alerted the international media about the sporadic but systematic killings that were going on around Nyamata. As a result, the international media descended on Nyamata and reported the killings. The police commander was so infuriated by the presence of the international media that he shot Tonia Locatelli. She is buried at the side of the church.

Locatelli's story becomes even more significant in the light of the events of 1994, when following the UN order to airlift for-

---

[15]Esquivel, *Threatened with Resurrection*, 63.
[16]Ibid., 61.

eign nationals from Rwanda, the missionary priests and nun at Nyamata who were protecting tens of thousands of Tutsi refugees in the church compound, were evacuated, and immediately thereafter, the Interahamwe militia killed more than 2,000 refugees in the church compound.

The fact that Toni Locatelli lies buried in Nyamata alongside other (Rwandan) victims of genocide not only redefines the concept of "my people," it announces her resurrection into a new communion beyond black and white. That is why in a world marked by neat and settled identities of race, gender, nation, and tribe that divide Christians, we need her story. For without a story like hers, we lose the ability to imagine, dream, and live into the reality of the church as a resurrected and "strange" communion of witnesses drawn from all tribes, nations, and languages.

Naming and Remembering Martyrs

Neither Locatelli nor Mujjawamaholo has been officially declared a martyr by the Catholic Church. That I nevertheless have been referring to them as martyrs is not only an indication that I use the designation of martyr in a somewhat loose sense; I am also suggesting that a recovery of the gifts of martyrs has to do with the recovery of a vibrant conversation about why and who the church should name as martyrs.[17] If such a conversation becomes dull or uninteresting, then the church is in danger of losing the skills and courage necessary for the Christian journey. But it is also obvious why the church might be unable or even reluctant to engage the conversation about martyrs in a lively and ongoing way. For doing so involves accepting and welcoming the threat that martyrs offer. In that case, the church is much safer without the stories of the martyrs. And yet, as I have shown, without martyrs, the church would not be able to name the gift of God's peace in the world, nor the shape of the journey this gift involves.

I am also suggesting that a recovery of the gifts of martyrs has

---

[17]I therefore find Robert Royal's book *The Catholic Martyrs of the Twentieth Century* (New York: Crossroads, 2000) very helpful in engaging this conversation—not only because of its attempt to provide a global map for martyrdom in our time, but also for the stories and lives he names as martyrs, some of them controversial.

to do not only with the practice of naming martyrs, but also with the rich tradition of remembering martyrs. Such remembering takes many forms: vigils, feast days, storytelling, renaming, etc. It is through these practices that martyrs are remembered by the church. But it is through such remembering that the church itself is re-membered as community across the divisions of race, tribe, and nation, and constituted as a pilgrim people—a people on a journey toward the peace of God's new creation. A church that does not have the tradition and practice of honoring martyrs not only lives in the ever-present preoccupation of its projects; such a church soon loses the skills to name the gifts of God's peace and the habits that sustain the journey.

PART III

IMPROVISING NEW CREATION

*On Being Ambassadors of Reconciliation
in a Divided World*

8

Archbishop John Baptist Odama and the Politics of Baptism in Northern Uganda

My tribe is humanity.
—Archbishop Odama

The Coming of the Third Church

When I think about the discourse of Catholicity in our time, two words come to mind: ecology and *Kairos*. Both words point to the Global South as the locus of a renewed and fresh conversation about Catholicism in its methodological, hermeneutical, and ecclesiological dimensions. Using the story of Archbishop John Baptist Odama, I would like to provide an example of how a fresh conversation in the new era of world Catholicism around these three sites might look like.

John Allen is right. The "most rapid, and most sweeping, demographic transformation of Roman Catholicism in its two-thousand-year history"[1] is under way. Even if numbers tell only part of the story, they confirm the shift in the center of gravity of Christianity from its traditional heartlands in Europe and the United States, to the Global South of Africa, Asia, and Latin

---

Originally written for the "The Discourse of Catholicity," World Catholicism Week, Center for World Catholicism and Intercultural Theology, DePaul University Chicago, April 12–13, 2011.

[1]John Allen, *The Future Church: How Ten Trends Are Revolutionizing the Catholic Church* (New York: Doubleday, 2009), 17.

America, leading to the projection that by year 2025 only one Catholic in five in the world will be a non-Hispanic Caucasian.[2] What Philip Jenkins says of Christianity in general is particularly true of Roman Catholicism: "If we want to visualize a 'typical' contemporary Christian, we should be thinking of a woman living in a village in Nigeria or in a Brazilian *favela*."[3]

Even though the effects of this demographic transformation may yet be unclear, there seems little doubt that this historical moment—what Walter Bühlmann predicted as "The Coming of the Third Church"[4] or what Allen calls the "The World Church"—is ushering in changes that are not simply additive, but ecological.[5] That is why the shift in Catholicism's center of gravity raises not only methodological questions (the way Catholic theology as a disciplined inquiry is pursued), but questions about Catholic identity and theology in general. In the wake of the transformation, the discourse on Catholicity cannot proceed as usual, that is, neither from within the same location of the Global North, in the same methodological directions, nor with the same assumptions and questions. Instead, the discourse must be grounded within the

---

[2]"At the dawn of the twentieth century, there were roughly 266.5 million Catholics in the world, of whom over 200 million were in Europe and North America and just 66 million were scattered across the entire rest of the planet. Most of this remainder was in Latin America, some 53 million. The cultural and ethnic profile of the Church in 1900 was not terribly different from what it had been during the Council of Trent in the sixteenth century.

"In 2000, by way of contrast, there were slightly under 1.1 billion Roman Catholics in the world, of whom just 350 million were Europeans and North Americans. The overwhelming majority, a staggering 720 million people, lived in Latin America, Africa, and Asia. Almost half the Catholic total, over 400 million people, lived in Latin America alone. Projecting forward to the year 2025, only one Catholic in five in the world will be a non-Hispanic Caucasian" (Allen, *Future Church*, 17).

[3]Philip Jenkins, *The Next Christendom* (New York: Oxford University Press, 2007), 1–2.

[4]Walter Bühlmann, *The Coming of the Third Church* (Maryknoll, NY: Orbis Books, 1977).

[5]John Allen notes, "The late American cultural critic Neil Postman once famously argued that technological change is not additive, but ecological: that is, it doesn't just change one thing, it changes everything. Judging from its impact across wide range of issues in Catholicism, the emergence of a World Church is exactly like that. It is not merely adding something new to the life of the Church, but rather driving a holistic transformation, turning it upside down in virtually every area" (*Future Church*, 32).

experience, reality, and life challenges of the "typical" Catholic, and explore from within its world the pressing questions and fresh possibilities of what it means to Catholic.

Another way to make this claim is to note that the transformation of Catholicism currently under way presents a unique moment—a *kairos* (in the sense of a dangerous opportunity)—that not only raises a number of new questions but unsettles and reformulates hitherto established convictions and practices. It is important, however, to remember that whereas the transformation at hand might be the "most rapid," it is not the first time that Catholicism finds itself within such a moment. For as Dana Robert, the Truman Collins Professor of World Christianity and History of Mission at Boston University, notes, these historical moments happen "every time the gospel message makes itself at home among a new group of people."[6] This was particularly the case in the early church when Christianity first moved out of its Jewish home and became a predominantly Gentile religion. This cultural transition precipitated a crisis. "That so many non-Jewish believers were responding to the work of Paul and the other evangelists created a crisis for the original believers in Jerusalem, who sensed themselves losing control over the boundaries of the faith."[7] But it is this same cross-cultural process that resulted in what the missiologist Andrew Walls has famously come to describe as the "Ephesian moment"[8]—the coming together for the first time of Jewish and Gentile Christians around the meal table—two communities historically separated, sharing communion together as a sign of their "belonging together" as members of the same Body of Christ. Thus, for Walls as for Robert, the cross-cultural crisis was the unique opportunity for Christianity to become a "catholic" faith. Robert notes:

> The cross-cultural spread of the message, including translating it into terms that made sense to a Gentile audience,

---

[6]Dana L. Robert, *Christian Mission: How Christianity Became a World Religion* (Malden, MA: Wiley-Blackwell, 2009), 14.

[7]Ibid., 14.

[8]Andrew Walls, "The Ephesian Moment: At a Crossroads in Christian History," in Walls, *The Cross-Cultural Process in Christian History* (Maryknoll, NY: Orbis, 2002), 72–81.

set a pattern that not only separated Christianity from its Jewish background, but created a religion able to transcend cultural differences. The crucial decision to allow Greeks to become Christians and remain within their own cultural framework was the key that opened the future of Christianity to its global potential as a "world" religion, rather than remaining as a sect within Judaism.[9]

In our time, Catholicism finds itself within a similar cross-cultural moment. There is, therefore, a lot to learn from this early moment: from the questions it raised; the challenges it posed to Jewish Christians, who until then thought of the faith as their heritage; and the tentativeness with which new approaches, formulations, and doctrines were proposed and eventually adopted. The early Christian councils—from the council of Jerusalem during the time of the apostles, through Nicea (325), Constantinople (381), Ephesus I (431), Ephesus II (449), Chalcedon (451), and up to the Second Council of Constantinople (553)—not only bore witness to the process of theological exploration and innovation under way, they also were attempts to work through the theological, social, doctrinal, and political implications of the cross-cultural ferment. That out of this ferment emerged some of the clearest and richest expressions of Christian doctrine confirm Andrew Walls's remark about theology as a hazardous business, "'an act of adoration fraught with the risk of blasphemy' . . . [that] develops and grows in situations of crisis and urgency."[10]

The current cross-cultural transformation brings Catholicism within a similar dangerous but exciting moment of theological exploration, innovation, and experimentation. As Catholicism makes its new home within the so-called Global South, it is encountering new questions from Catholics who are often negotiating multiple sets of intersections: both from their inherited cultural and spiritual heritage and from the pressing social political cal exigencies of their postcolonial history. And that the world of the "typical Catholic" is by and large characterized not only by a primal spiritual outlook (which is far different from the Western

---

[9]Robert, *Christian Mission*, 14.
[10]Walls, *Cross-Cultural Process in Christian History*, 45.

secularized outlook) but also by the ongoing realities of poverty, violent disruption, war, famine, disaster, and displacement makes the Global South a lively laboratory, in which new pastoral and theological approaches in Catholic theology are being worked out. For, to the extent that the true origins of theology lie "not in the study or library, but from the need to make Christian decisions—decisions about what to do, and what to think . . . the normal run of Western theology is simply not big enough for Africa, or for much of the rest of the non-Western world."[11]

That is why a discourse on Catholicity must travel south in order to locate itself within the ferment of the cultural, pastoral, and theological synthesis under way within Catholicism itself. Doing so will not only help illumine fresh dimensions of Catholic identity and performance, it will hopefully also bring the Catholic Church within a new Ephesian Moment of full catholic communion, where the "very height of Christ's full stature" (Eph 4:13) might be revealed.

Traveling south is therefore what I want to do in this essay by telling the story of Archbishop John Baptist Odama of Gulu in Northern Uganda. Doing so allows me to highlight some of the pressing issues and challenges that face the typical Catholic in Africa as well as the resources Catholicism provides within this context. Accordingly, my overall aim is to show Archbishop Odama as, first, an exemplary case of Catholic improvisation, and second, to confirm the Global South as the site for a renewed and fresh conversation of Catholicism in its methodological, hermeneutical, and ecclesiological dimensions.

Archbishop John Baptist Odama and the Politics of Baptism

John Baptist Odama is the Catholic archbishop of Gulu, an archdiocese in Northern Uganda.[12] For a number of years, since

---

[11]Andrew Walls, "Afterword: Christian Mission in a Five-hundred-year Context," in *Mission in the 21st Century: Exploring the Five Marks of Global Mission*, ed. Andrew Walls and Cathy Ross (Maryknoll, NY: Orbis Books, 2008), 203.

[12]I have known John Baptist Odama since 1990, when he was appointed as the rector of Alokolum Seminary near Gulu. Because during this time, due to the insecurity in Northern Uganda, the seminary had been closed and the seminarians relocated to the sister seminary of Katigondo, where I was on faculty, Odama and I served together on the joint faculty of the two national seminaries. My

Yoweri Museveni came to power in Uganda in 1986, Gulu has been the epicenter of the civil war that has pitted Museveni's government in Kampala against the fighters of the Lord's Resistance Army (LRA) led by Joseph Kony. When Odama became archbishop of the newly created Archdiocese of Gulu in 1999, the civil war was at its height. The fighters of the Lord's Resistance Army (often referred to as "the rebels") waged war by not only ambushing government and military vehicles but also by attacking villages, burning down houses, abducting children (in all over 26,000 children were abducted), and ambushing, killing, and maiming civilians, thereby exercising over Gulu and the surrounding districts of Northern Uganda a "sovereignty of terror."[13] The government's offensive ("Operation Iron Fist," which began in 2002) against the rebels tragically resulted in more retaliatory attacks and eventually led to the government policy of confinement, forcing more than 90 percent of the population (1.8 million people) to become internally displaced persons (IDPs). Having little or no access to their fields and living in poor sanitary conditions, the population was reduced to a desperate situation of mere survival within the camps, where, additionally, alcoholism and prostitution became rampant, and the camps themselves became easy targets for the rebels.

This is the context into which Odama became archbishop of Gulu—a predominantly Catholic part of Uganda—a context of civil war that has defined his pastoral leadership. In 2006, after twenty years of armed conflict, a ceasefire between the Ugandan government and the LRA brought an end to the fighting (although Kony refused to sign the agreement, the LRA withdrew from Northern Uganda to the North of Congo and Chad). Archbishop Odama was instrumental in the peace process, working quietly behind the scenes to mediate between Museveni's government and Kony's LRA, traveling a number of times into the bush to meet with Kony and his commanders; appealing to and pressuring

---

reconstruction of his story is based on personal conversations as well as on two formal interviews during the 2009 Pilgrimage of Pain and Hope, July 29, 2009 (hereafter Gulu, July 2009), and more recently, at the Great Lakes Initiative (GLI) Institute at Ggaba on January 17, 2011 (hereafter Ggaba, January 2011).

[13]For a more extended discussion of Kony's sovereignty of terror in Northern Uganda, see my *The Sacrifice of Africa* (Grand Rapids, MI: Eerdmans, 2010), 148–65.

them to stop the fighting and then appealing to and pressuring the government to give up the Operation Iron Fist and agree to talks with Kony; serving as a strong advocate for the displaced people, children in particular; and finally helping to establish the ARLPI (Acholi Religious Leaders Peace Initiative), an advocacy group made up of Protestant, Catholic, Muslim, and traditional leaders working for peace, of which Odama became the chairperson and chief spokesperson.

For his work, Archbishop Odama and the ARLPI have received a number of international awards and recognitions.[14] Whereas these awards confirm Odama's extraordinary public leadership and advocacy, they do not explain the theological visions as well as the "inner" spiritual and devotional matrix[15] that grounds his leadership. However, attending to this matrix confirms that it is the Catholic tradition and faith in which Odama firmly stands that has not only opened up resources for his extensive social, pastoral, and activist innovation in dealing with the situation in Northern Uganda but has also grounded his struggles and leadership in a story beyond geographical boundaries. Four dynamic elements within this matrix deserve special attention:

A Universal Community and Identity

A vision of universal humanity rooted in God lies behind Odama's life and work in Gulu. He loves to speak of a foreign visitor who asked him about his tribe and to whom he responded, "My tribe is Humanity." In the way Odama tells the story he notes how the visitor, like many Western visitors to Africa who are so preoccupied with locating Africans within tribes, misunderstood "Humanity" to be the name of a particular tribe, and so followed up with a question by inquiring which region of Uganda this tribe was located in! Odama's point was not simply to show how so many Western visitors are locked into a

---

[14]The Niwano Peace Prize (Japan, 2004); The Paul Carus Award (Spain, 2004); the United Religions Initiative (URI) Africa Peace Award (Ethiopia, 2008); and more recently, the Breaking of Borders Award (San Diego, 2010).

[15]Todd Whitmore, "My Tribe Is Humanity: An Interview with Archbishop John Baptist Odama of Uganda," *Journal for Peace and Justice Studies* 20, no. 2 (Fall 2010): 61–75.

particular way of thinking about Africa, but, more important, to encourage a new way of seeing and relating. "We must all learn," he notes, "to see beyond tribe, race, and nation—and recognize that we are first and foremost human beings created in the image of God."[16]

It was Odama's Catholic upbringing and training for the priesthood that opened up and gradually led him to discover this universal dimension. Gulu is not Odama's native home, and Acholi is not his native tongue. He was born and raised in Arua (West Nile), went to seminary in southern Uganda, and graduated from the university in Kenya. Through these experiences of always living outside his home, Odama learned to see the world as one human family. In a July 2009 interview, he noted that his life has been "one long journey of conversion"—from "a local understanding of human beings to the sense of humanity."[17] His work as archbishop in Gulu has undoubtedly deepened this sense of belonging to a wider community that extends beyond Africa, and this is what he was pointing to when he said, "My people where I was born can no more contain me now. I am beyond their capacity."[18] Indeed, this has proved literally true, for his leadership in Gulu during the most challenging time thrust him into the national and international spotlight, as a result of which he has visited capitals around the world (the day he spoke at the Great Lakes Initiative [GLI] Institute in Kampala he was traveling to London for a two-day meeting). Therefore, it is not surprising when he says, "I find myself at home wherever I go. I am not a stranger. The world is my home.[19]

Beyond his own world travels, Odama's words point to the need to resist the entrenched forms of tribalism through which we tend to view those different from ourselves as strangers. We are not strangers, Odama insists, but fellow human beings created in the image of God. Moreover, for Odama it is not simply his cross-cultural experience that has brought him to this realization—it is a realization that is inexorably connected to his Catholic identity

---

[16]Interview with author, Gulu, July 2009.
[17]Ibid.
[18]Ibid.
[19]Ibid.

and the unique gift of baptism. Baptism locates one within a community that extends far beyond one's place of birth and makes one at home among people whom one has not yet met. This is the sense of baptism that Odama was invoking when, at the GLI Institute in January 2011, he told the story of when he was appointed rector of Alokolum. On his first visit to the seminary in 1990, speaking through an interpreter, he told the small group of village people who came to meet him, "You do not know me, but I am not a stranger. Do not call me a stranger. I am Ugandan, so are you, I am a Catholic, so are you; to go even deeper, I am a human being, so are you. So do not call me a stranger or foreigner here." He then added that "no child baptized within the Catholic Church should be called a foreigner in any place where there are Catholics." It was baptism into the Catholic faith that opened up for Odama this universal dimension of humanity.

Local Places and the Least of These (ngini ngini)

If Odama's baptismal journey has been a journey of conversion from a local to a global vision of humanity, it has also ironically led him to a deeper identification with the local places where he finds himself on his journey. He told the 2011 GLI participants that "whenever, I go to a new place, the first thing I do is learn the local language; acquire a taste for local food, attend local functions and celebrations in the village." Quite often, he noted, on realizing that "I am one of them, the people have often responded by giving me a local name."

What is perhaps most notable about Odama's identification with the local places is the identification with the most neglected and abandoned places—villages in Africa are seen in this way. "Village" does not name so much a place as a state of abandonment and neglect—the antithesis of modernity—which represents all that is backward in Africa. To aspire to modernity and civilization in Africa is to aspire to move away from the village, and everything that "village" represents, toward enlightenment and progress that "towns" and "cities" are supposed to represent. Odama's identification with villages and other abandoned places thus places him in a movement of countermodernity. When he was made bishop of the newly created diocese of Nebi in 1996, he made a point to visit the more than one hundred village chapels of his new diocese and spend at least two nights in each village, and in this way be became known as a "village bishop." Even as archbishop of Gulu and chairperson of Uganda Episcopal Conference, Odama still wears the simplicity of a country pastor.

It is the identification with the village as a form of the most neglected that explains Odama's special love for children, who within the context of war in Northern Uganda are quite often the most abandoned and abused. Odama has given the children a nickname—"ngini ngini"—which in Luo is the name of the tiny ants that are almost invisible and are thus readily stepped on and crushed. For Odama to call the children "ngini ngini" is a sign of his endearment to the "most precious, weak, and vulnerable creatures of God." Whenever Odama comes to a village, the ngini ngini run to him, flock around him, and hold onto his purple robes. As he leaves, they run after his car, waving and calling out "ngini ngini"—an interesting reversal that seems to suggest that the children themselves have come to recognize the archbishop, this mighty, strong, and powerful man, as also a weak, precious, and a vulnerable creature of God.

It is this universal image of humanity, as lived out within the local village and abandoned places and individuals, especially children, that lay behind Odama's fierce determination to end the civil war, as well as his efforts toward a comprehensive peace solution in Northern Uganda.

The Task: "Redeeming This Place"

As archbishop of Gulu, Odama understands his task in very specific and concrete terms as one of "redeeming this place." When he was appointed the rector of a seminary that had been looted and abandoned, he invited the residents of Alokolum to work toward a collective goal:

> I am not a stranger. I am one of you. We are going to work together. This is our common ground. The seminary is our common ground. And you and I have to cooperate to redeem this place, and bring back life and [the seminarians] to *this* place. (Ggaba, January 2011)

In the context of Northern Uganda, the task has been made particularly urgent by the reality of the ongoing war between the government and the rebels of the Lord's Resistance Army. Odama was not only committed to end the war, but to building a peaceful society where the full humanity of the child can flourish. No better image captures this commitment than when, during his speech at his installation as archbishop of Gulu, he put aside his prepared script, took a child in his arms, and asked the child, "Do you like war?" The child turned his head from side to side in a gesture to signify "no." Odama then asked the child, "Do you like peace?" to which the child nodded a very enthusiastic "yes." Then Odama, still holding the child in his arms, turned to the audience and said, "This child has defined for us our pastoral ministry. I commit myself to work for the future, which this child has defined, to eliminate war, build peace . . . so that the full humanity of this child might grow and flourish."[20]

What this image confirms is that the politics that drives Odama is local (redeeming "this place"); its requirements very specific ("we must end the war"); and extremely urgent (the future of children, the "ngini ngini," is at stake). It is this very local, concrete, and urgent task that led Archbishop Odama into all forms of advocacy, which have included drawing on the global contacts of his Catholic world to advance the search for peace in Northern Uganda. At the height of the Lord's Resistance war, he traveled often to the Vatican, Europe, and the United States, where he connected with Catholic networks, institutions, and movements and enlisted their support. However, even as these contacts around the world are vital to his work, the one most critical to his mission is not a *local, not even global contact, but one beyond* this world.

Thursday as a Day of Adoration

Even as Odama stands firmly within the local politics of Northern Uganda, and in the specific and urgent exigencies of ending the war, the politics that informs, drives, and directs his efforts comes from beyond this place. This is what is reflected in

---

[20]Ibid.

Odama's practice of setting Thursday aside as a day of prayer, fasting, and adoration. Asked why he takes this day off, Odama noted, "So that I may not take myself too seriously. The mission of peace is not mine. I do not own it. It is owned by God, and I am merely the servant. . . . Many times I do not know the next steps toward peace, but I know that steps to peace can be found."[21]

At the GLI Institute, he explained his Thursday practice in terms of "reporting." "He [God] is my boss. God is the one who has given me this. I see this as God's mission. The mission of peace is of Christ, is of God. On Thursday, I take to him what is going on; what is happening."[22] He also explained that what he is doing when he is alone before the Blessed Sacrament is listening. It is this listening, he noted, that keeps him hopeful in the face of so much suffering and the apparent lack of positive results in the efforts for peace: "This time keeps me focused and I 'listen.' . . . In this way, I can remain hopeful. For I hear God saying, 'Do not lose hope. Do not be afraid. I am with you always.' "

Pressed on why he needs a whole day to do this, he responded: "Connecting with God takes time."[23] Moreover, this is also the time when he connects with humanity most intimately:

> I pray for all humanity. I bring all of . . . humanity before God. As I bring my hands and fingers together (representing all continents, male and female in creation), I say, "I am an ambassador for all these people in front of you." I represent all their needs. (Gulu, July 2009)

It is interesting that Odama uses the language of "ambassador"— a reference to 2 Corinthians 5:20: "So we are ambassadors of Christ since God is making his appeal through us." That text comes toward the end of Paul's statement about new creation: "If anyone is in Christ, there is a new creation; everything of old has passed away; the new is here; *all this is from God*" (2 Cor 5:17–18). It is this decisive understanding of new creation—as a gift from God—that is at the heart of Odama's Thursday practice. For even as the task of redemption (redeeming this place) does

---

[21]Ggaba, January 2011.
[22]Ibid.
[23]Ibid.

indeed require tireless effort and advocacy, in the end it is a gift from God. Accordingly, Odama can say, "The mission of peace is not mine. I do not own it. It is owned by God, and I am merely the servant," and that is why he must take a whole day off, to listen, to connect, to wait for, and to learn to receive the gift of peace—not just for the place called Northern Uganda, but for himself as well. Understood from this point of view, Odama's Thursday practice is not an interruption of or even a rest from his advocacy, it intensifies it. His Thursday practice is the politics of redeeming a local place par excellence, of receiving the gift of new creation, and of working as an ambassador for a new future, which only God can realize.

I have taken the time to tell the story of Archbishop Odama so as to depict the kind of everyday challenges faced by today's typical Catholic. But I also hoped to show the kind of resources, visions, and innovations that Catholicism makes available in the context of those challenges. In this case, hopefully Odama's story provides an exemplary case of Catholic performance in the Global South. But my hoped in telling the story of Archbishop Odama in the way I have done was also to help me identify sites around which a fresh discourse on Catholicity can be generated in the era of world Catholicism. Three sites are particularly worth noting.

Reframing the Discourse on "Catholicity": Three Sites

Methodology: Global Ethnography

One reason I have felt it necessary to tell the story of Archbishop Odama has been to model the kind of theological ethnography that this unique moment of Catholic history calls for. The era of a world church provides a wonderful opportunity to tell stories of Catholic performance from around the world—stories that illumine what Catholicity is about, display the difference Catholicism makes around the world, and capture something of the catholicity of Catholicism.[24] For such narratives from around the world not only provide contrasting perspectives of

---

[24]Margarita Mooney's *Faith Makes Us Live: Surviving and Thriving in the Haitian Diaspora* (Berkeley: University of California Press, 2009) exemplifies the type of theological ethnography to which I am pointing.

catholicity, they also lend greater insight into the whole, into connections, disconnections, and reconnections. Without stories like that of Odama, a discourse on Catholicity runs the danger of degenerating into a debate about "positions" of assumed spiritual, moral, or doctrinal orthodoxy, or, even worse, being sucked into the intractable cultural wars between the Right and the Left of Western political and religious agendas.

Hermeneutic: The Politics of Baptism

The coming to be of the Third Church also provides us with a moment to recover a simple starting point in the discourse of Catholicity. When Pope Paul II visited France in 1981, he asked the French bishops and delegates, "Are you faithful to the promises of your baptism?"[25] This question could serve as a good starting point, suggesting baptism as a hermeneutic point of reference in a renewed conversation about Catholicity. In this connection, a conversation of catholicity framed around the notion of baptism can be particularly helpful in engaging questions about identity in the face of growing forms of tribalism. For, despite what is often celebrated as the amazing benefits of globalization that are purportedly making the world a small village, the world of the twenty-first century has become increasingly tribal, with ethnic, religious, racial, national, and economic disparities creating wedges between peoples. A renewed conversation about baptism as an invitation and initiation into a new way of being in the world can offer resources for learning to think and live beyond tribe, race, and nation. In this connection, Odama's story as a journey of "conversion from a local to a universal" sense of community and belonging points to the true gifts of catholicity that baptism opens up. Pope Benedict is thus right when, as Cardinal Ratzinger, he noted that, thanks to baptism, there are no strangers in the church:

> Everyone in it is at home everywhere. . . . Anyone baptized in the church in Berlin is always at home in the church in

---

[25] "Allow me . . . to question you: 'France, eldest daughter of the Church, are you faithful to the promises of your baptism?'" As quoted in George Weigel, *Witness to Hope: The Biography of John Paul II* (New York: HarperCollins, 1999), 377.

Rome or in New York or in Kinshasa or in Bangalore or wherever, as if he or she had been baptized there. He or she does not need to file a change-of-address form; it is one and the same church. Baptism comes out of it and delivers [gives birth to] us into it.[26]

This is exactly the sense of catholicity that Odama is acting out of and driving toward. But what Odama's story also reveals is the expansive sense of belonging that baptism offers, which stretches beyond any tribal, ethnic, or national community by locating one within a community capable of exploding even the boundaries of the "Catholic" community so as to reveal a truly catholic community as the destiny of all God's children. That is why Odama can say "my tribe is humanity." That is the end, the telos, to which baptism points.

Ecclesiological Ruminations: The Church on Its Knees

Odama's story offers a number of ecclesiological ruminations. My favorite image of Odama shows him kneeling before children during the 2009 Peace Week, when he commits to serve the *ngini ngini* during his tenure as archbishop. This incident had the same effect as an earlier incident when Odama had knelt before the children to ask for their forgiveness, on his behalf, on behalf of the religious leaders, and on behalf of all adult members of the community who had let the war drag on, thereby sacrificing the future of the children.[27] The images of Odama on his knees surrounded by children are powerful. However, to get the full ecclesiological force of these images they must be related to another

---

[26]Statement made in a letter of the Congregation for the Doctrine of the Faith quoted in an article by Cardinal Joseph Ratzinger, "The Local Church and the Universal Church: A Response to Walter Kasper," *America* 185, no. 16 (2001): 11. For a more extended discussion of the implications of this sense of "belonging," see my review of Lamin Sanneh's *Whose Religion Is Christianity? The Gospel beyond the West*, *Pro Ecclesia* 15, no. 1 (2006): 140–45.

[27]This earlier incident occurred in 2003 when Archbishop Odama, together with the other leaders of ARLPI, slept in a marketplace in Gulu in solidarity with the "night commuters"—children who at the height of the war feared being abducted and who would therefore leave their homes in the evening and "commute" to Gulu town to sleep in the open.

picture of Odama on his knees—on Thursday, in adoration in his chapel. These images belong together and illumine in a vivid way the nature, identity, and mission of the church in the world.

The church is called to be sign and sacrament of God's new creation in the world. The preeminent modalities of this mission are service, forgiveness, and ambassadorial advocacy. Seen from this angle, it becomes clear that what Odama is driving at in all advocacy and engagement—or what is driving Odama—is a practical ecclesiological vision, which is to say, a vision of the church in the business of redemption. This mission is not abstract. It is always local, specific, and urgent, and always engaged from the vantage point of the "least of these." The essential marks of service, forgiveness, and advocacy are intimately tied together and together radiate the story of God who came to "dwell among us," thereby inviting us into a new community of humanity-with-God, in which our true identity as God's children can both be revealed and flourish.

Caught in the intractable debates framed by Right or Left religious agendas, in the entrenched positions of moral, spiritual, or doctrinal orthodoxy, or in the power and numbers game of "whose turn" it is (to govern, or exercise power), it is easy to forget this simple vision of the call and mission of the church in the world. A discourse on Catholicity in our time becomes an opportunity to rehearse what might appear to be simple, and yet the most critical, questions for a renewed conversation about Catholicity: What is the church? Why is the church needed in our time, and how can the church live into that mission within a given location in the world? Because stories like that of Archbishop Odama illuminate these ecclesiological dimensions, they make the discourse of Catholicity interesting, and thus offer a fresh confirmation of why and how the church is needed both as the recipient of God's gift of new creation and as its ambassador in a broken and violent world.

9

Archbishop Emmanuel Kataliko and the "Excess of Love" in Bukavu

If politics is trying to win by making the other person look worse off, then I will never be a politician. . . . But if politics is building schools, if politics is setting up infrastructures getting to make sure that everybody has certain rights like education and health—if politics is trying to optimize what you have in the system in terms of public resources, then that's the kind of politics I would like to do. And I am already a politician in that sense.

—Davis Karambi

The logic of the Gospel is a logic not of power, but of the cross. . . . The only response to the excess of evil is the excess of love.

—Emmanuel Kataliko

On Christmas Day 1999, as the Rwanda-backed Rally for Congolese Democracy (RDC) controlled South Kivu, Archbishop

---

An earlier version of this essay with the title "The Gospel as Politics in Africa: An Excess of Love in the Midst of Africa's Turbulent Social History," was read at XXXVII Settimana europea di Storia religiosa, Le missioni in Africa: La sfida dell'inculturazione, Villa Cagnola a Gazzada (Varese), September 2–5, 2015. It was revised and published as "The Gospel as Politics in Africa," *Theological Studies* 77, no. 3 (2016): 704–20. Reprinted here with permission.

Emmanuel Kataliko of Bukavu preached a sermon in which he denounced the "empire of greed" and the "insatiable thirst for material things" that fueled the war, looting, and violence in Eastern Congo:

> We are crushed by the oppression of domination. Foreign powers in collaboration with some of our Congolese brothers, organize wars with resources of our country. These resources, which should be used for our development, for the education of our children, for healing the sick, in short, so that we may live more humanely, are used to kill us. Moreover, our country and ourselves, we have become objects of exploitation worse than the colonial era. . . . Everything of value has been looted, wrecked and taken abroad or simply destroyed. Taxes, which would be invested for the common good, are misappropriated. . . . Excessive taxes strangle not only large-scale commerce and industry, but also the mother who lives off her small business. . . . In the city armed groups, often in military uniforms, burst into our houses, steal the few goods we have left, threaten, kidnap and even kill our brothers. Our brothers and sisters in the countryside are massacred on a large scale. . . . Even the church is not spared. . . . Parishes, presbyteries, convents are sacked. Priests, clergy, and nuns are beaten, tortured and killed. . . . The moral decline of some of our compatriots has reached such an absurd level, that they do not hesitate to betray their brother for a bill of ten or twenty dollars.[1]

I begin by drawing attention to Archbishop Kataliko's famous Christmas message because it captures well the context, possibilities, and urgency for the New Evangelization (NE) in Africa. Kataliko's sermon highlights the challenge of political violence in Africa and locates the need for New Evangelization within the context of the search for a different, nonviolent basis for society in Africa. Because this particular need, as well as the overall political crisis of Africa, has not been fully attended to, given the

---

[1]See Emmanuel Kataliko, "Lettre de Noel 1999," in *Lettres pastorales et messages de Monseigneur Emmanuel Kataliko (18 mai 1997–4 octobre 2000)* (Bukavu: Editions Archevêché Bukavu, n.d.), 80–83 (translation mine).

cultural emphasis within the project of the New Evangelization, Kataliko's story offers an opportunity to reaffirm a comprehensive vision of reconciliation as the goal of the New Evangelization in the context of Africa's turbulent history.

My argument progresses in four sections. In the first section, I trace the development of the project of the New Evangelization so as to highlight its cultural emphasis. In the second section, I show that the faith crisis in Africa is neither primarily nor predominantly cultural, but rather political—specifically it has to do with the ongoing phenomenon of political violence, which is traceable to the colonial heritage and imagination of Africa's modernity. Given this foundational story, the missiological and theological challenge has to do with the search for a fresh vision—a different, nonviolent basis of a new African society. In the third section I register that although the search for a new social vision for Africa was noted by the second African synod, the post-synodal apostolic exhortation *Africae Munus (AM)* stopped short of offering reconciliation as the comprehensive vision for a nonviolent foundation of society. In the fourth and last section, I argue that it is the search for a nonviolent basis for social existence that was at the heart of Kataliko's life and ministry in Eastern Congo. In the conclusion, I draw implications from Kataliko's life and message in Congo for what the Gospel can offer in the context of Africa's social political history. In this connection, I note the similarity between Kataliko's vision of the Gospel as an "excess of love" and Pope Francis's vision of mercy as "the beating heart of the Gospel."[2] At the basis of both Kataliko's and Francis's messages is a dynamic spiritual encounter, which cannot but be political at the same time in that it calls for nothing short of new social relationships and possibilities that reflect God's merciful and reconciling love.

New Evangelization: A Cultural Emphasis

When John Paul II first proposed the project of the New Evangelization it was in response to a perceived cultural prob-

---

[2]Pope Francis, *Misericordiae Vultus* (*The Face of Mercy*), Bull of Indiction of the Extraordinary Jubilee of Mercy (2015), https://w2.vatican.va.

lem mostly affecting Christianity in the West—those "countries and nations where religion and the Christian life were formerly flourishing" but are now being "put to a hard test" and in some cases have been "even undergoing a radical transformation, as a result of a constant spreading of religious indifference, secularism and atheism."[3]

Thus, in an address to the church in Europe, John Paul II noted the "urgent need for a 'new evangelization,' in the awareness that 'Europe today must not simply appeal to its former Christian heritage: it needs to be able to decide about its future in conformity with the person and message of Jesus Christ.'"[4]

Pope Benedict XVI followed John Paul II in highlighting the cultural problem of secularism and religious indifference affecting Western churches. And even though Benedict was able to extend the call for new evangelization to the churches in Africa and Asia, the impetus behind this call was that even these "young" churches were, because of increasing globalization, faced with similar cultural challenges. Thus, in proclaiming a Year of Faith, creating a Pontifical council for the Promotion of New Evangelization, and calling a special synod to coincide with the fiftieth anniversary of the beginning of Vatican II, Benedict proposed the New Evangelization as a project for the whole church, which finds itself within a new "cultural environment":

> New evangelization is precisely the Church's ability to renew her communal experience of faith and to proclaim it within the new situations which, in recent decades, have arisen in *cultures*. The same phenomenon is taking place in both the North and South and the East and West; in both countries with an age-old Christian tradition and countries which have been evangelized within the last few centuries. The coalescing of social and *cultural* factors—conventionally designated by the term "globalization"—has initiated a process which is weakening traditions and institutions

---

[3]See John Paul II, Post-Synodal Apostolic Exhortation *Christifideles laici* (1988), 34. See also Synod of Bishops, XIII Ordinary Assembly, The New Evangelization for the Transmission of the Christian Faith, *Instrumentum Laboris* (2012) (hereafter *IL*), 13.

[4]Cited at *IL*, 45.

and thereby rapidly eroding both social and *cultural* ties as well as their ability to communicate values and provide answers to perennial questions regarding life's meaning and the truth. The result is a significant fragmentation of *cultural* unity and a *culture's* inability to hold fast to the faith and live the values inspired by it.[5]

I highlight the "cultural" emphasis in this formulation because it helps show the relation between faith and culture as the immediate challenge that the call to New Evangelization addresses. As the synod on the New Evangelization noted: "NE calls for particular attention to the inculturation of faith that can transmit the Gospel in its capacity to value what is positive in every *culture*, at the same time, purifying it from elements that are contrary to the full realization of the person according to the design of God revealed in Christ."[6] Although this is no doubt the case, the cultural emphasis in the project of the New Evangelization has meant that the political context of evangelization has not received as much attention. This is especially true in relation to Africa, where the New Evangelization has been dominated by issues of inculturation and African culture. The discussion by Father Bede Ukwuije provides a most illuminating confirmation.[7] In a highly lucid and informative essay delivered to the General Assembly of Africans and Malagasies at the Service of the Generalates in Rome (May 25, 2013) he notes that "the renewal of faith in Africa has to take the cultural crisis Africa is going through seriously. This cultural crisis has to do with the crisis of meaning, which is embodied in different realities, more especially in ethnocentricism, the explosion of witchcraft and the subtle spread of secularism, propagated by the development of functional religion."[8] He proposes the need for the New Evangelization "to embark on a critical inculturation which will involve the rethinking and transformation of African cultures."[9]

---

[5]*IL*, 47 (emphasis mine).
[6]*Synodus Episcoporum Bulletin: XIII Ordinary General Assembly of the Synod of Bishops*, Oct. 7–28, 2012, Proposition 5, http://www.vatican.va.
[7]Bede Ukwuije, CSSp, "Faith in Africa in the Context of the New Evangelisation," May 25, 2013, http://www.sedosmission.org.
[8]Ibid., 212.
[9]Ibid., 218.

I do not deny that ethnicity, witchcraft, and the subtle spread of secularism are major challenges in Africa. Neither do I deny that a rethinking of African cultures is necessary. My concern, however, is that characterizing the crisis of faith in Africa as primarily a cultural crisis tends to obscure the social political context of modern Africa, more specifically the reality of political uncertainty and violence across much of the continent. In fact, I believe that more than any cultural challenges, it is the political culture of violence in which African Christians experience and live their faith that provides the most critical challenge to the Gospel. This of course is not to deny the need of the New Evangelization in Africa. It is to locate the need and urgency of the New Evangelization within a fresh vision of the Gospel and of a new African society. This is what Emmanuel Kataliko offered to the people of Eastern Congo through the story of a God who responds to evil and violence through "the excess of love." Such message, as we will see, not only would have far-reaching social implications but also points to a vision of society grounded in nonviolence. In order to appreciate the at once fresh and radical nature of Kataliko's message, one has to locate it against the background of Africa's social history, which has been marked by violence.

The Sacrifice of Africa: Salvation from King Leopold's Ghost?

Political uncertainty, violence, and insecurity are endemic in much of postcolonial Africa. The Rwanda genocide of 1994, which killed close to a million people, is still a fresh memory. Closer in time, civil wars in Sierra Leone, Ivory Coast, Southern Sudan, and the Central African Republic have displaced millions and left thousands dead. More recently, the crisis of President Nkurunziza's third-term project in Burundi has sent tens of thousands of Burundians into exile, and left millions fearing a return to the genocidal wars of a decade or so earlier. Although these may appear as isolated incidents, they reveal something of the underlying imagination that drives politics in modern Africa, where the competing economic and political interests of a limited elite shape a social history of poverty, civil wars, abuse of basic rights, and a general sense of desperation and helplessness. Within this context, millions of young, vulnerable, unemployed youths become an easy target for recruitment or abduction into the militia forces. And as is often the case in Africa, the fighting sooner or later takes on an "ethnic" dimension. But as I have argued elsewhere, ethnicity is not the major problem in Africa. The problem of ethnicity has to do with the underlying visions of society, identity, and well-being that drive modern Africa, within which the realities of violence, ethnicity, and poverty are perpetually reproduced.[10]

Recent developments in Congo confirm this conclusion. With more than 30 million Catholics (over 60 percent of the population), Congo has the largest Catholic population in Africa. But for the last twenty-five years, this second largest African country, the size of Western Europe, has been the center of a series of wars and fighting that have left millions displaced from their homes, more than 5.4 million dead; tens of thousands of women raped,[11] and its 67 million people among the world's impoverished.

It is not easy to untangle the complex set of factors, motivations, and history of what has come to be known as the "Congo Wars," which at their height involved the armies of nine countries, multiple groups of UN peacekeepers, and over twenty armed groups. However, in *Dancing in the Glory of Monsters: The Collapse of the Congo and the Great War of Africa*, Jason Stearns provides some good anchors and a helpful starting point. He offers a vivid and moving chronicle of the Congolese Civil Wars, which began in 1996 in the wake of the Rwanda genocide, and which brought to an end Mobutu's thirty-one-year reign and the installation of Laurent-Désiré. What I find particularly helpful in *Dancing in the Glory of Monsters* is not only that it sheds light on the key actors (especially Rwanda and Uganda), their complex

---

[10]See the full argument in my *The Sacrifice of Africa: A Political Theology for Africa* (Grand Rapids, MI: Eerdmans, 2011).

[11]A 2011 study in the American journal of *Public Health* indicated that 1,152 women were raped every day—a rate equal to 48 per hour (cited in Jo Adetunji, "Forty-eight Women Raped Every Hour in Congo, Study Finds," *Guardian,* May 12, 2011, http://www.theguardian.com. The study, carried out by three public health researchers from the International Food Policy Research Institute at Stony Brook University in New York, and the World Bank, showed that 3 percent of women across the country were raped between 2006 and 2007, and that 12 percent of all women had been raped at least once.

calculations and agency during the war, but also and even more important that Stearns is able to locate the fighting within the context of Congo's political history.

It is Congo's social history that accounts for the fragile nature of the state. As Stearns notes:

> Since 1970 until today, the Congolese state has not had an effective army, administration, or judiciary, nor have its leaders been interested in creating strong institutions. Instead they have seen the state apparatus as a threat, to be kept weak so as to better manipulate it. This has left a bitter Congolese paradox: a state that is everywhere and oppressive but that is defunct and dysfunctional.[12]

However, the institutional weakness of the Congo state does not reflect a "failed" state; it is a reflection of the colonial legacy according to which Congo was turned into the private business empire of King Leopold—a policy that was continued by the Belgian government and by Mobutu after that. In other words, the institutional weakness of the state advances the politics of plunder and greed that has been from the beginning part of the imagination of modern Congo.

This is also greatly true about the reality of war and fighting in the Congo. The violence at the heart of Leopold's project has been well noted.[13] What now becomes clear in light of Stearns's book is that the senseless violence and massacres in the wake of the Congo Wars are a perpetuation of King Leopold's "rubber terror," even as they bring that violence to a new, unprecedented height. The new height was especially realized during the so-called second war (1998–2003) when the entire country, especially Eastern Congo, became militarized. At one point in the war between Kinshasa and Rwanda, Kabila dropped tons of weapons and ammunition at various airports in the jungles of the Eastern Congo for the Hutu militia as well as for other indigenous militia groups known

---

[12]Jason K. Stearns, *Dancing in the Glory of Monsters: The Collapse of the Congo and the Great War of Africa* (New York: Public Affairs, 2011), 126.

[13]Adam Hochschild, *King Leopold's Ghost* (Boston: Houghton Mifflin, 1998). See also my *Sacrifice of Africa* for a full discussion.

as *maji maji*.[14] Rwanda responded in kind. The result was that throngs of discontented and unemployed youth joined militias on either side of the proxy war. But instead of fighting a war, these militias simply "set up roadblocks to tax the local population." In the same way "family and land disputes, which had previously been settled in traditional courts, were now sometimes solved through violence, and communal feuds between rival clans or tribes resulted in skirmishes and targeted killings."[15] Soon governors created their own local militias. But instead of "improving security, these ramshackle, untrained local militias for the most part just exacerbated the suffering by taxing, abusing, and raping the local population."[16] It is within this context that one has to understand the ethnic dimension that the fighting in Eastern Congo would soon take on, especially in Ituri where Lendu and Hema tribes slaughtered each other with reckless abandon.

We have found it helpful to briefly draw attention to Stearns's *Dancing in the Glory of Monsters* so as to highlight the social history within which the violence in Congo, including the "ethnic" conflict between the Hema and Lendu becomes thinkable. To abstract the conflict from the wider history and turn it into a problem of ethnicity is to fail to understand it, but it is also to misleadingly focus on African culture as the problem. But we have also drawn attention to the story of the Congo because it provides a glimpse into the kind of political imagination that drives much of Africa. For in many ways, Congo serves as a mirror to African society. To use Frantz Fanon's famous image: "Africa has the shape of a pistol, and Congo is the trigger. As goes the Congo, so goes the rest of Africa."[17]

We have drawn attention to the story of the Congo also because it helps to put the missiological and theological challenge into sharp focus. For given the social history, the same question

---

[14]Stearns, *Dancing in the Glory of Monsters*, 250.

[15]Ibid., 250–51.

[16]Ibid., 251.

[17]Quoted ibid., 45 (see Frantz Fanon, *The Wretched of the Earth* [New York: Grove Press, 1963]). See also Michela Wrong, who describes Congo as a "paradigm of all that was wrong with post-colonial Africa," even as Congo has taken all the contradictions and faults of any normal African country and brought them to their logical extremes (*In the Footsteps of Mr. Kurtz: Living on the Brink of Disaster in Mobutu's Congo* [New York: HarperCollins, 2001], 10).

that was put to the missionaries at the height of Leopold's rubber terror in the Congo, namely whether the Christian savior had any power to save from King Leopold's rubber terror, is the same challenge confronting Christianity in Africa today.[18] This is the question that makes the project of the New Evangelization urgent in Africa given the widespread violence across the continent. But if my argument is correct that the imagination of violence is wired within the imaginative landscape of modernity in Africa, then the need for the New Evangelization is not simply a quest for new strategies and skills to help manage the violence in Africa. It is a quest for a new political imagination, which is to say a quest for a different vision of society than the violent and self-serving "politics of the belly" that drives much of modern Africa. For as Jean-Marc Ela had already noted in the 1980s, the mission of the church in Africa must be placed within the context of the search "for another history, another society, another humanity, another system of production, another style of living together."[19] And while the need for a new social history in Africa was noted by the Second African Synod, the latter stopped short of offering the Gospel as the foundation for a new history. That this was the case had partly to do with the worry of getting the Gospel too much entangled in politics. But as Kataliko's life and message will confirm, the Gospel is inevitably political. The decisive question is the kind of politics that the story of God's love shapes.

The Search for Another (Hi)story: Promises and Limitations of *Africae Munus*

Both the second synod of bishops for Africa and the post-apostolic exhortation *Africae Munus* (*AM*) acknowledged that the New Evangelization "is an urgent task for Christians in Africa because they too need to reawaken their enthusiasm for being members of the church" (*AM*, 171). The need for the New Evangelization was affirmed against the backdrop of Africa's political crisis, which was noted by the synod:

---

[18]See my *Sacrifice of Africa*, 20.
[19]Jean-Marc Ela, *My Faith as an African* (Maryknoll, NY: Orbis Books, 1988). 84.

The thirst for power leads to contempt for all the elementary rules of good governance, takes advantage of people's lack of knowledge, manipulates political, ethnic, tribal and religious differences and creates cultures where warriors are considered heroes and people need to be paid back for past sacrifices and wrongs committed.[20]

It is within this context that *Africae Munus* noted the "anthropological crisis" (11) arising in part out of "Africa's painful memory of fratricidal conflicts between ethnic groups, the slave trade and colonization." Given this crisis "that has left Africa painfully scarred," Pope Benedict reaffirmed:

What Africa needs most is neither gold nor silver. She wants to stand up, like the man at the pool of Bethzatha. She wants to have confidence in herself and in her dignity as a people loved by her God. It is this encounter with Jesus which the church must offer to bruised and wounded hearts yearning for reconciliation and peace, and thirsting for justice. (*AM*, 9)

I read this conclusion by Pope Benedict as a confirmation of the urgent need for a new story in Africa, one that "heals, sets free, and reconciles" and thus is able to engender, in the already cited words of Jean-Marc Ela, "another history, another society, another humanity, another system of production, another style of living together." The various recommendations of *Africae Munus* for the African church to pursue reconciliation should accordingly be seen as a constitutive dimension of this quest for another vision of sociality in Africa. For as Benedict notes, "Evangelization today takes the name of reconciliation, 'an indispensable condition for instilling in Africa justice among men and women, and building a fair and lasting peace that people of good will irrespective of their religious, ethnic, linguistic, cultural and social backgrounds'" (*AM* 174).

Although these indications seem to suggest reconciliation as the foundation for a new political vision for Africa, there is a fundamental tension in *Africae Munus* that leads to hesitations and in

---

[20]*IL*, 11.

some instances even a pulling back away from a comprehensive vision of reconciliation in favor of a more standard approach. The hesitation is evident on at least two levels. First, although *Africae Munus* issues an explicit appeal for the church and Christians "to pursue" reconciliation, justice, and peace, it does not provide a comprehensive framework that displays reconciliation as a "gift"—God's gift to the world, to Africa in particular. Accordingly, the preoccupation with the church's mission and with pastoral guidelines and strategies in *Africae Munus* easily leads to an impression that reconciliation is just one pastoral agenda among many—although an urgent and timely one. A final message from the synod confirms this by urging bishops "to put issues of reconciliation, justice and peace high up on the pastoral agenda of their dioceses."[21]

But reconciliation is not just another priority area of the church's mission. It is God's gift of "new creation" to the world (2 Cor 5:17)—and an invitation to enter and experience the world of new creation, which God has made possible through God's reconciling love. For as Paul says, "If anyone is in Christ, the new creation has come: The old has gone, the new is here! All this is from God, who reconciled us to himself through Christ (2 Cor 5:17–18). In the context of Africa's turbulent political history, the invitation offers not simply concrete alternatives to violence, but a basis for a new society founded on God's nonviolent and reconciling love.

The second area where *Africae Munus* seems to pull back from a dynamic vision of reconciliation as the basis of a new society in Africa is in the sharp distinction that Benedict draws between the spiritual and political realms. I suspect that he does so in order to protect the call for reconciliation from sounding too political. For instance, even as he notes that reconciliation is of great importance to the task of politics, he qualifies the statement by noting that reconciliation itself "is a pre-political concept and a pre-political reality" (19). He also rightly notes that the Gospel brings about a "revolution," but immediately qualifies, stating that "Christ does not propose a revolution of a social and political kind, but a revolution of love brought about by his complete self-giving through

---

[21]*Message to the People of God of the Second Special Assembly for Africa of the Synod of Bishops*, 19, http://www.vatican.va.

his death on the Cross and resurrection" (26). Even as the pope offers recommendations to Christians at various levels of society to take their faith seriously as the foundation for building a just and peaceful African society, he says that "the building of a just social order is part of the competence of the political sphere" (22) and warns that "the church's mission is not of a political nature." Its task is "to open the world to the religious sense by proclaiming Christ" (23). Throughout *Africae Munus* Benedict tries to walk a tightrope between a vision of reconciliation in its holistic and revolutionary dimension and a spiritual vision of reconciliation, based on the realization that the political realm lies outside the church's competence.[22] The tension remains unresolved, even though in the end, in an interview after the closing Mass at the synod (October 26, 2012), Benedict pointed to pastoral praxis as the ground where the full implications of a Christian vision of reconciliation are worked out:

> A pastor's language, instead, must be realistic, it must touch upon reality, but within the perspective of God and His Word. Therefore this mediation involves, on one hand being truly tied to reality, taking the care to talk about what is, and on the other hand, not falling into technically political solutions: this means to demonstrate a concrete but spiritual world.[23]

The attention to pastoral praxis is a welcome one. For attending to the pastoral praxis within the historical context of Africa

---

[22]In an interview after the closing Mass at the synod (October 26, 2012, Rome), and in *Africae Munus* 17, Pope Benedict points to the tension: "The theme 'reconciliation, justice, and peace' certainly implies a strong political dimension, even if it is obvious that reconciliation, justice, and peace are not possible without a deep purification of the heart, without renewal of thought, a 'metanoia' without something new that can only come from the encounter with God. But even if this spiritual dimension is profound and fundamental, the political dimension is also very real, because without political achievements, these changes of the Spirit usually are not realized. Therefore, the temptation could have been in politicizing the theme, to talk less about pastors and more about politicians, thus with a competence that is not ours. The other danger was—to avoid this temptation— pulling oneself into a purely spiritual world, in an abstract and beautiful world, but not a realistic one" http://www.vatican.va.

[23]*Address of His Holiness Benedict XVI during Luncheon with Synod Fathers* (October 24, 2009), https://w2.vatican.va.

not only confirms the need and urgency of a new political imagination, it also confirms that the "revolution of love, brought about by his [Jesus'] complete self-giving through his death on the Cross and his resurrection" (*AM*, 26), totally reshapes the social and material conditions of a society. This is what makes the Gospel good news in the context of Africa's turbulent political history, which calls for a new social imagination. It is this search for a new, nonviolent basis for society that drove Kataliko's ministry in the Congo. And so, in order to explore the full political implications of the New Evangelization as reconciliation, we need to attend to his story.

Kataliko and an "Excess of Love" in the Congo

Emmanuel Kataliko was installed as archbishop of Bukavu in May 1997 at a very turbulent time in Congo's political history. His predecessor, Archbishop Christopher Munzihirwa, had been assassinated seven months earlier. It was two days after Mobutu fled Kinshasa and two days before Laurent-Désiré took power. A year later Kabila would fall out with his Rwanda and Uganda allies, plunging the Congo into the second Congo War.[24] The Rally for Congolese Democracy (RCD), a Rwanda-sponsored rebel group, controlled Bukavu and the whole of Southern Kivu and was exercising heavy taxation on the city. Overall, by 1999, the economic, political, and security situation in and around Bukavu was becoming dire. Numerous Maji Maji groups (local indigenous militias) had formed. Massacres were common, as were pillage and looting. It was against this background that Kataliko preached his famous 1999 Christmas message denouncing Rwanda's occupation and the "empire of greed," and "the insatiable thirst for material things" that fueled the violence and looting in Eastern Congo.

Kataliko's sermon struck a chord not only with Catholics in Bukavu, but with Protestants, Muslims, and the entire civil soci-

---

[24]For more on this history, see John Kiess, *When War Is Our Daily Bread: Congo, Theology, and the Ethics of Contemporary Conflict* (PhD diss., Duke University, 2011), http://dukespace.lib.duke.edu. I am particularly indebted to Kiess, who first drew my attention to the story of Emmanuel Kataliko, and whose work provides in the story and leadership of Kataliko a most compelling account of Christian agency, reasoning, and alternatives in the midst of fighting.

ety of Bukavu. A one-week strike was called to protest the high taxes levied by the RCD and the continued presence of Rwandan and Ugandan forces in Eastern Congo. The strike closed schools, health clinics, NGO offices, markets, and transportation, and thus brought the city to a halt. The RCD responded by arresting Kataliko and exiling him to Butembo, his former diocese, accusing him of political involvement, inciting civic unrest, and promoting ethnic divisions.

In accusing Kataliko of political involvement, the RCD wanted him to stick to his "pastoral duties" and care for the "spiritual needs" of the people. Kataliko insisted that that was exactly what he was doing.[25] And so, even from exile, he continued to write pastoral letters to his congregation. However, from these letters it becomes obvious that even though Kataliko never described his ministry in political terms, the message of Christ crucified that he shared with the people was in itself a deeply subversive political message, in that it invited Christians into a different vision of politics and of society than the one pursued by the RCD and the other warring factions. No doubt it was a profound spiritual message about the story of God's excess of love manifested on the cross. In a Lenten message from Butembo (March 15, 2000), Kataliko wrote:

> In these difficult times, let us not doubt the love of God for us. "If God is on our side, who will be against us?" (Rom 8:31–9). But know the logic of the Gospel is a logic not of power, but of the cross. "God has chosen the weak of the world to undermine the strong" (1 Cor 1:27). The only response to the excess of evil is the excess of love.[26]

The excess of love that Kataliko notes here is the logic of the cross. This for Kataliko is the way that God responds to evil, suffering, and violence in the world, by his willingness to become a victim rather than a perpetrator of violence. God conquers the violence of the world through suffering. In his Lenten letter the previous year, Kataliko wrote of God's suffering servant of Isaiah (50:6–7):

---

[25]See *Les écrits . . . de Mgr Kataliko*: Textes rassemblés et présénts par: Daniel Kamable Kombi, Agustin Kahindo Snege et Jean-Piere Kabuyaya Mbeva (Kinshasha: Kombi and Sons, 2000), 41–49.

[26]*Les écrits . . . de Mgr Kataliko*, 50.

Although wounded, he did not wound others. Although he was subjected to injustice, he did not respond with injustice. Although he was humiliated he did not humiliate those who were weaker than himself. Although he was suffering, he resisted, keeping in his heart the dream of a society founded in justice, without oppressor or any oppressed. (Is 42:2–4)[27]

As this statement shows, the dream of God's suffering servant is at the same time a unique social vision, a vision of society "founded in justice, without oppressor or any oppressed." Jesus as God's suffering servant confirms this vision of "crucified love" as the basis of our life in God and with one another. Kataliko continues in the same Lenten message:

In this lifelong battle, He knows that in this world justice and love cannot exist unless they are crucified. He thus accepted to be hung on the cross, this instrument of torture reserved for slaves that the son of God transformed into a means of liberation and redemption. His courage came to Him in the certainty that to live with love, to practice justice, and to tell the truth is the only way to have God on your side.[28]

Kataliko drew from this realization that it is through this "crucified love" that God "reconciles" the world to Godself—inviting fallen humanity into God's love even as God stands in solidarity with suffering humanity. In doing so, Jesus becomes the source and model of all our human and material engagements, and for this reason, the practical dimensions of everyday life are not outside the story of God's love for humanity; they are a reflection and an extension of God's love and solidarity. This explains Kataliko's own passionate concern for human dignity and for "development." When he was bishop of Butembo, he was personally involved in the building of roads, bridges, schools, hospitals, and a university. And when he was transferred to Bukavu, in his very first pastoral letter (1997) he mobilized the population to

---

[27]"Courage, j'ai vaincu le monde" (Jn 16, 33): Lettre pastorale de Carême 1999, in *Lettres Pastorales et Messages de Monseigneur Emmanuel Kataliko* (18 mai 1997–Octobre 2000) (Éditions Archeveche Bukavu, 2000), 58.

[28]"Courage, j'ai vaincu le monde," 58.

repair the city drainage. The practical and mundane concerns were part and parcel of the logic of the excess of love.

But in the same way that the practical details of life are not merely mundane matters, so the church's spiritual and liturgical practices are not merely spiritual or pious exercises. They are concrete opportunities that introduce and form Christians into the story of God's reconciling love. For Kataliko, therefore, liturgical practices and seasons are a way of entering into this different, nonviolent logic—God's way of responding to evil with an excess of love; they are an invitation into a different history—for Kataliko, the true and only history of the world. Entering this different (hi)story is what allows one to see that for all their pretensions, it is not Kabila, Kagame, Kagutu, or the generals that controlled Congo's history, but the crucified God. Accordingly, the different liturgical seasons of Advent, Christmas, Lent, and Easter became opportunities for Kataliko to narrate the fighting christologically (thus his pastoral letters) and situate the crisis in Bukavu within the wider drama of the Incarnation.[29] Moreover, it was the renewal of this narration that allowed Kataliko to see clearly and name different forms of "servitude" (plunder, violence, greed, oppression, etc.) in the Congo; it also revealed concrete options and practical alternatives to resist such various forms of servitude. Thus, in his September 1998 pastoral letter, he offered these practical alternatives:

> In the face of violence, let us endeavor to resist with all the strength of our faith, without letting ourselves be taken in by an equal spirit of violence. . . . In the face of poverty that weakens us, react with an effort made in solidarity. In the face of famine that threatens us, let us strive to respond with an even greater engagement in work, without letting ourselves be paralyzed by fear and lassitude. . . . Everyone should

---

[29]As John Kiess notes, Kataliko does not approach the war as a separate sphere of human action with its own time and law, but instead shows how the church's liturgical time of birth, passion, and resurrection remains the determinative lens for Christians throughout rebel occupation (*When War Is Our Daily Bread,* 150). As the season of Advent transitions to Lent, Kataliko moves from the theme of birth, which sprung the church into action on the streets of Bukavu, to the theme of suffering and the church's entry into the paschal mystery of Christ (ibid., 168).

work to make sure they meet the needs of their families. . . .
Merchants should not succumb to the temptation to profit
from the general distress by raising prices of essential goods;
farmers should redouble efforts . . . to cultivate the fields
and thus produce the necessary food for their subsistence
and that of their brothers and sisters in the city.[30]

These concrete alternatives constitute for Kataliko "the work
of peace," which does not wait till the end of the war, but goes
on as everyday work even in the middle of the war. What is significant, of course, is that for Kataliko these are not free-floating
strategies of peace building. They are the practical, social, and
political implications of the story of God's excess of love.

Let me close by highlighting four implications that emerge from
this discussion that confirm the immense political possibilities of
the Gospel in the context of Africa's social history.

First, what the discussion of Kataliko makes obvious is that
even though Kataliko understood the Gospel as a spiritual message about God's excess of love that led Jesus to the cross, he
understood this message to be at the same time the primary lens
through which to understand our lives here and now. The story
not only provided the interpretative lens through which Kataliko
read the history of Congo but also shaped his life as a pastor. It lay
behind his interest and involvement in various efforts for human
development in Butembo and drove his passionate advocacy on
behalf of the embattled people of Bukavu. In the latter case, the
story not only offered courage to denounce the greed that fueled
the fighting in Eastern Congo, it opened up concrete possibilities
of nonviolent alternatives, which he offered to the people. That
the alternatives he offered were concrete and specific confirms that
for Kataliko the Gospel did not exist in its own sublime realm
of only spiritual matters but was and is always incarnated in the
messy world of particular histories and contexts. Perhaps this is
what Pope Benedict had meant by noting that a pastor's language
must be realistic and thus "demonstrate a concrete but spiritual

---

[30]Kataliko, "Soyez forts et courageux," in *Lettres Pastorales*, 27–28.

world."[31] However, because his thinking held a neat distinction between the religious and the political realms, Benedict could not envisage, in the same way that Kataliko did, a whole new social reality being opened up by the story of God's reconciling love. What Kataliko's message shows is that when one stands within the story of God's reconciling love, the very boundaries between religion and politics are put into question.

Second, although the generals might have been right to accuse Kataliko of meddling in politics, they completely underestimated the kind of politics that the story of God's excess of love had opened up for Kataliko. The generals viewed Kataliko's engagement from a narrow partisan lens (and saw him as a politician), but Kataliko was involved in a far more subversive political project. His project involved nothing less than a redefinition of politics from the vantage point of the story of God's nonviolent and reconciling love. The immediate social and practical implications of this redefinition was that for Kataliko politics was not about power in the sense of domination, force, and plunder, but power as self-sacrificing service on behalf of others. This is the sense of politics that Davis Karambi, a young Kenyan who helped his village build a sustainable education fund, is referring to when he notes:

> If politics is trying to win by making the other person look worse off, then I will never be a politician. . . . But if politics is building schools, if politics is setting up infrastructures to make sure that everybody has certain rights like education and health—if politics is trying to optimize what you have in the system in terms of public resources, then that's the kind of politics I would like to do. And I am already a politician in that sense.[32]

This is the kind of politics that Kataliko pursued. But for Kataliko, of course, this vision of politics and his engagement of it

---

[31]*Address of His Holiness Benedict XVI during Luncheon with Synod Father* (October 24, 2009).

[32]Davis Karambi, cited in Dayo Olopade, *The Bright Continent: Breaking Rules and Making Change in Modern Africa* (Boston: Houghton Mifflin Harcourt, 2014), 213.

was simply an outworking of the practical implications of the story of God's excess of love within a particular time and place. For a people trapped in a social history of violence, looting, and exploitation, Kataliko's politics offered not only language to name their servitude but also possibilities for nonviolent forms of engagement, solidarity, and peaceful coexistence. It is therefore not surprising that Kataliko's message struck a chord not only among Catholics but also among Muslims, Protestants, and the entire civil society of Bukavu.

Third, that Kataliko's message struck a chord beyond the Catholic community reveals interesting parallels between Kataliko and Pope Francis. Even though Pope Francis has not adopted New Evangelization as the banner of his pontificate, he has provided a fresh vision of the Gospel and the urgent work of evangelization in our time through his focus on mercy. Mercy, he has noted, is "the beating heart of the Gospel," the "bridge that connects God and man, opening our hearts to a hope of being loved forever despite our sins."[33] But just as Kataliko was to discover in the story of God's excess of love, a rich social and political vision, the story of God's mercy foregrounds Francis's ecclesiological vision and dynamic social political engagement. Comparing the church to a field hospital, Francis has noted, "This is the mission of the Church: to heal the wounds of the heart, to open doors, to free people, to say that God is good, God forgives all, God is the Father, God is affectionate, God always waits for us."[34] Behind this statement is the vision of the church as a redemptive community that heals social wounds and divisions. It is a similar sentiment that lies behind Francis's declaration of the Extraordinary Jubilee and Year of Mercy as an opportunity to reinvigorate the church in its mission as the sacrament of God's mercy in the world and to invite the church and humanity as a whole into a fresh experience of the richness of God's love and mercy in its spiritual, social, and political dimensions. The social and political implications of this invitation became particularly apparent during the pope's trip to Africa especially his visit to the war-torn Central African Republic (CAR). Whereas he spoke to

---

[33]Pope Francis, *Misericordiae Vultus*, 2.
[34]Pope Francis, "The Church Should Be Like a Field Hospital," Homily at Casa Santa Marta, February 5, 2015, http://www.romereports.com.

many audiences and offered numerous encouragements toward an end to violence and peace in CAR, none was as powerful as when he opened the Holy Door of the Immaculate Conception Cathedral at Bangui on November 29, 2015, for the beginning of the Jubilee of Mercy. This marked a first time for the Jubilee Holy Door to be opened outside Rome, and the fact that this was ten days before the formal opening of the Jubilee of Mercy in Rome on December 8, made the event at Bangui even more significant. It confirmed Francis's vision that God's mercy was not simply a sentimental consolation or mere spiritual platitude, but the most decisive intervention and alternative to the madness of war. "The Holy Year of Mercy comes early to this land," Pope Francis told the gathered congregation, "a land that has suffered for many years."[35] During the homily, he reminded the congregation that one of the many gifts of God's merciful love is that it invites us to love our enemies, "which protects us from the temptation to seek revenge and from the spiral of endless retaliation."[36] He then appealed to Christians to live out this Gospel of mercy: "In every place, even and especially in those places where violence, hatred, injustice and persecution hold sway, Christians are called to give witness to this God who is love." Although in the cathedral Francis spoke mostly to Christians, he carried the same message of peace grounded in the story of God's mercy in his meeting with Muslim and evangelical leaders: "To those who unjustly use the weapons of this world, I launch this appeal: Lay down those instruments of death. . . . Arm yourselves instead with justice, love and mercy, the authentic guarantors of peace."[37] In this connection, he paid tribute to an interfaith platform created by the archbishop, the imam, and the pastor in Bangui,[38] whose efforts were also recognized by the United Nations.[39]

---

[35]"The Pope opens the Holy Door of Mercy in Bangui, 'Spiritual Capital of the World,'" *News.Va*, November 30, 2015, http://www.news.va.

[36]Pope Francis, "Homily, Mass with Priests, Religious, and Seminarians, Immaculate Conception Cathedral," November 29, 2015, Vatican Press Office, http://www.ewtn.com.

[37]Ibid.

[38]For more on the Central African Interfaith Peace Platform, see http://www.c-r.org. See also http://worldea.org.

[39]See "Interfaith Peace Platform Wins UN Peace Award," Conciliation Resources, August 2015, http://www.c-r.org.

There are a number of similarities that one can draw between Kataliko's "excess of love" and Francis's "Gospel of Mercy" that confirm the inherent political character of the Gospel. On the plane back to Rome from the Central African Republic, a reporter asked Pope Francis whether his tribute to the interfaith peace platform meant that religious leaders should intervene in the political sphere. Francis's response: "Intervening in the political sphere: if that means 'being a politician,' then no. Let them be a good priest, imam, or rabbi: that is their vocation. But in an indirect way we do get involved in politics when we preach values, true values."[40] In Francis's response is the realization, which Kataliko's life and message confirm, that the more the religious leaders contemplate and take seriously their religious calling and message, the more they are able to discover its rich political potential. What both Kataliko and now Francis show is that the story of God's excess of love (Kataliko) and mercy (Pope Francis) offers not simply skills, techniques, and motivations to manage the current political realities, but the possibility to "cross over to another shore"[41] (Francis) and thus enter into a completely different story, one that engenders a different politics, or in the memorable words of Jean-Marc Ela, a "different world right here."[42] In an Africa dominated by the politics of power struggles, violence, and all forms of exclusion, there seems to be no more urgent task than inviting African peoples into a different history. This is the task that calls for New Evangelization efforts on the continent, for which Kataliko and Pope Francis provide compelling examples.

---

[40]In-Flight Press Conference, November 30, 2015, http://www.ewtn.com.

[41]Pope Francis, Homily, Mass with Priests, Religious, and Seminarians, Immaculate Conception Cathedral, November 29, 2015.

[42]Jean-Marc Ela, *African Cry* (Maryknoll, NY: Orbis Books, 1986), 53.

10

A Blood Thicker Than the Blood of Tribalism

Maggy Barankitse's Maison Shalom

William T. Cavanaugh's work has had a decisive influence on me and my attempt to understand the complex challenges related to nation-state politics in Africa and the difference that Christianity, Catholicism in particular, makes in responding to these challenges. When I first discovered Cavanaugh, through his book *Torture and Eucharist*, it was immediately clear to me that what Cavanaugh said about torture in Pinochet's Chile had immediate implications for Africa. In fact, the insights from *Torture and Eucharist* are what helped me to fully understand the violence during Idi Amin's regime in Uganda and to see how violence has been and continues to be a form of political imagination in much of modern Africa.[1] As

---

Originally given as a response to William Cavanaugh's keynote address, "The World Reconciled: Eucharist and Politics," at the World Catholicism Week, DePaul University, Chicago, April 16, 2012. Cavanaugh's paper has since been published as "The Church in the Streets: Eucharist and Politics," *Modern Theology* 30, no. 2 (April 2014): 384–402. A revised version of my talk was published, in the same volume of *Modern Theology*, as "A Blood Thicker Than the Blood of Tribalism: Eucharist and Identity in African Politics," *Modern Theology* 30, no. 2 (April 2014): 319–25. It is reproduced here, with slight revisions, with permission from the editors.

[1]See "Remembering Idi Amin: On Violence, Ethics, and Social Memory in Africa," in Emmanuel Katongole, *A Future for Africa: Critical Essays in Christian Social Imagination* (Scranton, PA: University of Scranton Press, 2005), 3–28.

I read Cavanaugh's essay "The World Reconciled: Eucharist and Politics," in which he explores the interconnectedness of Eucharist and politics through the work of Henri de Lubac, I see yet another feature of Cavanaugh's work that has deep relevance for Africa. For a key conclusion that emerges out of de Lubac's emphasis on the Eucharist as social and the Eucharist as action[2] is a vision of the Eucharist as a form of politics—a way of "configuring bodies in space, creating a large body politic" out of individual bodies ("World Reconciled," 3). Thus Cavanaugh writes:

> If politics is defined not as the achievement of state power but more broadly as the ordering of bodies in space and time, then we should be able to see how—as in Chile, Poland, the Philippines, and many other places—the church can enact Eucharistic bodies in space and time that stand as counter-politics to violence and injustice, while avoiding both Church-state entanglement, and the secularization and irrelevance of the Church in the West. (19)

In this brief reflection, I wish to build on this conclusion and show how the kind of Eucharistic theology and praxis that Cavanaugh outlines in this essay can help in addressing a major and ongoing social challenge in Africa, namely the challenge of tribalism.

Although almost everyone agrees that tribalism is a major problem in Africa, it is often not clear what tribalism is, or the sort of problem it is. In fact, part of the challenge of addressing tribalism in Africa has to do with the failure to grasp the unique reality of tribalism as a distinctly modern problem. For the usual assumption is that tribalism is a hangover from Africa's primitive past, arising out of Africa's diverse cultures, ethnicities, languages, and communities, which in the past either had nothing in common or lived in primitive warfare, which now have to learn to live together under the modern (nation-state) dispensation. What this prevalent view assumes is that "ethnicity" and "tribe" are simply given or natural categories (the way we were created)

---

[2]William T. Cavanaugh, "The World Reconciled: Eucharist and Politics," 2. Subsequent references are by page number within parentheses in the text.

about which nothing can be done. Moreover, the view assumes that the state is a benevolent or at least neutral actor whose role is to mitigate the tribal chaos and ensure peaceful coexistence through forms of cultural understanding and tolerance as well as other programs—of mediation, conflict resolution, reconciliation, etc.—to manage the occasional clashes and warfare between the different tribes.

This fairly standard way of understanding tribe and tribalism in Africa is misleading. First, tribe and ethnicity are as not as natural as we often think. As they operate within modern politics in Africa, these categories do not merely reflect a natural or even cultural form of belonging. They are rather forms of political identity,[3] which is to say (to use Cavanaugh's words) they are a "way of configuring bodies in space, creating a large body politic out of individual members" ("World Reconciled," 3). What this observation means in relation to Africa is that the modern political space (the nation-state) in Africa, is "imagined" and thus configured as a space, within which African individuals can be recognized and thus access political rights and privileges *only* as a member of a tribe or ethnic group, which group is at the same time set up in an imaginary competition with other tribes, whose members must be excluded from accessing what seem to be limited political rights and privileges. Thus, rather than being the savior from tribal chaos, the modern nation-state in Africa imagines and thus reproduces tribalism as an enduring feature of modern politics in Africa. By configuring African bodies as tribal entities, African politics opens up tribal sentiments and loyalties to the possibility of being constantly played and manipulated

---

[3]The Uganda social scientist, Mahmood Mamdani makes a crucial and helpful distinction between cultural and political identities. Cultural identities, Mamdani notes, are a "consequence of the history of development of communities that share a common language and meaning"—thus, a reflection of a shared *past*. Political identities, in contrast, arise out of a legal definition and are in view of a *future* political project. "If your inclusion or exclusion from a regime of rights or entitlements is based on your race, ethnicity, as defined by law, then this becomes a central defining fact for you the individual and your group. From this point of view, both race and ethnicity [and I should add tribe] need to be understood as political—and not cultural or even biological identities." See Mahmood Mamdani, *When Victims Become Killers: Colonialism, Nativism, and the Genocide in Rwanda* (Princeton, NJ: Princeton University Press, 1998), 58–59.

within the clientele politics of modern Africa. The tribalization of politics accounts for much of the violence in postcolonial Africa.[4] From a theological point of view, the far greater challenge arising out of the unique chemistry of tribal politics in the nation-state is the way the categories of tribe and ethnicity are framed as reflections of natural or biological identities, about which nothing much can be done. But framing these categories as natural simply seals them off from the supernatural realm, surrenders them to the temporal realm of politics, and prevents any possible reimagination or reconfiguration from a theological point of view. It is this assumption that makes it difficult for the church in Africa to challenge or provide viable alternatives to the phenomenon of tribalism in Africa. It is perhaps not difficult to understand why historically this has been the case, especially in light of Cavanaugh's essay. The evangelization of Africa, taking place in the wake of the European post-Enlightenment separation of church and state, and carried out by missionaries often operating out of a neo-Scholastic nature-grace distinction, positioned the church's competence within the spiritual realm, thereby surrendering the natural sphere to the realm of politics. This meant that missionary Christianity by and large located itself within the colonial imagination of African bodies and their configuration within the colonial regime as tribal individuals. And thus, even when evangelization was met with great success, as the case of Rwanda confirms, it was simply assumed that the church could not provide an alternative configuration of Rwandan society in terms of a new identity beyond Hutu and Tutsi, which had now come to be assumed as natural identities—identities that could not be altered. A Catholic identity in Rwanda was built on the identities of Hutu and Tutsi. But that baptism, church membership, and the sacraments including the Eucharist could do nothing to alter these so-called natural identities simply meant that Catholicism in Rwanda was built on the tacit, but heretical, acknowledgment that the blood of tribalism runs deeper than the waters of baptism. In this case, as in many others, Rwanda serves as a good mirror for much of Africa, as in much of Africa Christianity still operates

---

[4]For a more extended argument of this conclusion, see my *The Sacrifice of Africa: A Political Theology for Africa* (Grand Rapids, MI: Eerdmans, 2011), esp. 64–86.

out of the same neo-Scholastic, neocolonial legacy.[5] In the case of Rwanda, what the neo-Scholastic heritage meant was that far from being viewed as an action—indeed a way of reconfiguring individual bodies in the wider body politic called the church—the Eucharist was celebrated primarily as a means for individual piety. This explains some of the most bizarre incidents during the 1994 genocide, of Christians going to celebrate Mass in the morning before going out to hunt down and kill Tutsi neighbors![6]

But if we take de Lubac's insistence on Eucharist as action as well as his resistance against the reduction of the Eucharist to individual piety, then we can see how the Eucharist can serve as a form of counterpolitics to tribalism in Africa. In fact, it is something like de Lubac's re-centering of the church in the Eucharist that Pope Benedict drew on in the post-synodal Apostolic Exhortation, *Africae Munus*: *The Church in Africa in Service to Reconciliation, Justice and Peace* (*AM*), in calling for a new vision of African society beyond tribe and ethnicity: The pope stated, "We must really open these boundaries between tribes, ethnic groups and religion to the universality of God's love" (*AM*, 39)

Just as de Lubac insisted the supernatural is not separated from the nature, and the spiritual is always mixed with the temporal ("World Reconciled," 17), thereby asserting the church's eminence over everything, Pope Benedict in *Africae Munus* makes a similar claim. In calling for the realities of tribe and ethnicity to be "opened up" Benedict is pointing to the fact that these identities are not static or stable—in the sense of a natural essence. Neither are they an end in themselves. They remain open to reconfiguration and direction toward their true end, the universality of God's love. Moreover, even though for Benedict the word of God and the Eucharist are so deeply bound together that it is impossible to understand one without the other (*AM*, 40), Benedict, like de Lubac, notes that it is within and through the Eucharist, that the action of opening up and reconfiguring different cultures, tribes, and ethnicities to their true end is at once made possible and visible in the reality of the church as God's family: "The Eucharist is the force which brings together the scattered children of God and

---

[5]See my (with Jonathan Wilson-Hartgrove) *Mirror to the Church: Resurrecting Faith after Genocide in Rwanda* (Grand Rapids, MI: Zondervan, 2009).
[6]Ibid.

maintains them in communion, 'since in our veins there circulates the very Blood of Christ, who makes us children of God, members of God's Family'" (*AM*, 41). The image of the church as God's family was adopted by the 1994 synod as a compelling model for the church in Africa.[7] In using this image, Benedict is keen to show that the sense of family is not some ephemeral, mystical reality that hovers over the physical, temporal realm—but a real presence in the world, as both sign and sacrament—of the fact that the blood of Eucharist is thicker than any so-called natural identities of tribe and ethnicity:

> The most effective means for building a reconciled, just and peaceful society is a life of profound communion with God and with others. The table of the Lord gathers together men and women of different origins, cultures, races, languages and ethnic groups. Thanks to the Body and Blood of Christ, they become truly one. In the eucharistic Christ, they become blood relations and thus true brothers and sisters, thanks to the word and to the Body and Blood of the same Jesus Christ. This bond of fraternity is stronger than that of human families, than that of our tribes. (*AM*, 152)

One could dismiss this claim as utopian idealism if one did not have examples of communities such as Maison Shalom in Burundi, where something of a Eucharistic reconfiguring of tribal identities is under way. Having witnessed and escaped genocide in 1993 in which ethnic Tutsis killed over seventy-two Hutus, the founder of Maison Shalom, Maggy Barankitse (herself an ethnic Tutsi), gathered orphaned and abandoned children, both Hutu and Tutsi, and planned to raise the children beyond the hatred and bitterness that she had witnessed in the genocide.[8] For Maggy this meant trying to offer the children a new sense of identity beyond Hutu and Tutsi. Calling ethnicity a lie, she noted: "We are crazy. We are not afraid to kill one another. We have accepted hatred because of ethnicity and have forgotten the

---

[7]See the Post-Synodal Exhortation *Ecclesia in Africa*, 1994, http://www.vatican.va.

[8]For a more elaborate discussion of Maison Shalom, see Katongole, *Sacrifice of Africa*, 166–92.

most noble gift of belonging to the family of God."[9] In the story of God's love Maggy was to discover not only her own identity and calling, but a fresh experience of the reality of God's love, which she now offered to the children as the primary and by far more truthful account of their identity. She constantly reminds the children: "Each person is created in and out of love as God's child, and is meant to live in the house of God as a member of God's family."[10] For Maggy, the identity of being created in God's love is not an ephemeral experience, but a concrete lived reality, whose social, temporal, economic, and political dimensions she was determined to work out at Maison Shalom: setting the children up in homes, providing them with education, businesses, recreational facilities, etc.—while all along insisting that Maison Shalom is not about these projects—but about our identity as members of God's family, created in and out of love.

What lies behind Maggy Barankitse's determination to say No to the lie of ethnicity is the Eucharist, which is at once the sign and sacrament of the identity and experience of being part of God's family. In talking about the Eucharist, Maggy notes:

> Every morning we become new, because God creates us anew. And every time we go communion, we pray: "make us new" We go like this: [and she stretches out her hands as in receiving communion]. And when I go and take, I know that God cleanses my sins; God gives me another life, and then I can celebrate life all the day, all the night.[11]

At the 2008 49th Eucharistic Congress in Quebec, Canada, Maggy Barankitse reiterated the sense of new identity that the Eucharist creates and renews. She told the story of how she founded Maison Shalom and how she "put Hutu and Tutsi children together and Congolese children too, and I told the children, your ethnicity is called shalom."[12] Calling on the bishops and other delegates to "have courage to lose our heads in the

---

[9]Christel Martin, *La haine n'aura pas le derniere mot: Maggy la femme aux 10000 enfants* (Paris: Albin Michel, 2005), 47.
[10]Ibid.
[11]Personal interview, Ruyigi, January 2009.
[12]49th Eucharistic Congress, http://www.vatican.va.

Eucharist," she noted that losing our heads in the Eucharist is at once a rediscovery of our true identity and a way of seeing and living in the world. The Eucharist, she noted, "is a spirituality that includes everything."[13]

Although not using exactly the same words, Maggy Baran-kitse's vision of Eucharist as a "spirituality that includes every-thing" comes pretty close to Augustine's vision of "the world reconciled," of which the church is both sign and sacrament. The children at Maison Shalom, who have come to see themselves as neither Hutu nor Tutsi, but "Hutsitwacongozungu" (all ethnicities reconciled!) as well as Maison Shalom's programs in the remote village of Ruyigi—farms, guesthouses, a cinema, a swimming pool, a hospital, a mechanic shop, and so on—provide evidence and confirmation that the theological claim of a "world reconciled" is not simply a possibility, it is a reality. In this connection, Maison Shalom is the argument that proves that the blood of Eucharist is thicker than the blood of tribalism. At the same time it serves as a counterpolitics to the tribalism, violence, and poverty of Burundi's nation-state imagination. It is a clear exemplification of de Lubac's claim of Eucharist as action and Eucharist as politics.

---

[13]Ibid.

11

Field Hospital

The Compassion of Jo and Lyn Lusi in Eastern Congo

I find no better way to explore the theme of mission's critical and constructive engagement with societies, change, and conflict than to attend to the image of the church as a field hospital. Doing so helps make explicit the interconnections of evangelism, ecclesiology, and politics. The church, Pope Francis reminds us, is like a field hospital after battle, and as such, the church's unique location and mission is at the frontiers, where it enacts the social process of healing. Reminding us of the urgency of this call, Francis notes, "It is useless to ask a seriously injured person whether they have cholesterol and about the level of his blood sugars. You have to heal his wounds. Then you can talk about everything else. Heal the wounds, heal the wounds . . . and you have to start from the ground up."[1]

If the healing of wounds is the church's primary mission, it is at the same time the very message of her proclamation. For as Pope Francis notes, "The most important thing is the first proclama-

---

This paper was first given as a plenary address for the American Society of Missiology, St. Paul, Minnesota, June 17, 2016. A slightly revised version of the talk was published as "Field Hospital: HEAL Africa and the Politics of Compassion in Eastern Congo," in *Missiology: An International Review* 45, no. 1 (2017): 25–37. It is reproduced here with permission by the editors.
[1]Antonio Spadaro, Interview with Pope Francis, 2013, https://w2.vatican.va.

tion: Jesus Christ has saved you."[2] Elsewhere Pope Francis has noted that the content and object of the church's proclamation is God's mercy: "Mercy is the Lord's most powerful message."[3] This message is not simply pastoral, it is decisively political, and points to a vision of the church not so much as an institution, but as an event,[4] which in the very process of healing wounds, opens up fresh visions of what it means to be human—created in God's image—and initiates new social possibilities that reflect God's compassion in the world. Thus in healing wounds, the church offers to the world not simply forms of compassionate care; the church also gives birth to new social historical dynamics, which constitute a unique form of politics. As Francis notes:

> God manifests himself in historical revelation. . . . Time initiates processes, and space crystallizes them. . . . We must not focus on occupying the spaces where power is exercised, but rather on starting long-run historical processes. We must initiate processes rather than occupy spaces. God manifests himself in time and is present in the processes of history. This gives priority to actions that give birth to new historical dynamics.[5]

A number of questions arise here. For example, what does initiating new long-run historical processes mean? What do these new historical dynamics concretely look like? What constitutes their newness? How and in what way do they constitute a form of political engagement? These and similar questions lie at the heart of missiological research and reflection, which seeks to provide portraits of the church as a field hospital in its historical, pastoral, and political dimensions.

In this essay, I offer an example of the historical dynamics of healing wounds in Africa by telling the story of HEAL Africa in

---

[2]Ibid.

[3]"Mercy is the Lord's most powerful message" (Pope Francis, Homily Given at Sunday Mass, Santa Anna Church, March 17, 2013, https://w2.vatican.va.). See also Pope Francis, *Misericordiae Vultus* (2015), https://w2.vatican.va.

[4]For a full exploration of the social political implications of Pope Francis's ecclesiology of the field hospital, which informs my understanding here, see William T. Cavanaugh, *Field Hospital: The Church's Engagement with a Wounded World* (Grand Rapids, MI: Eerdmans, 2016).

[5]Spadaro, Interview with Pope Francis.

Eastern Congo. I do so not only to highlight HEAL Africa's political engagement in Eastern Congo as a model of mission's critical engagement with a wounded world, but to argue that mission's critical and constructive engagement with societies, change, and conflict takes the form of compassion. Thus, attending to HEAL Africa's compassionate engagement in Eastern Congo also helps illumine the church as a field hospital.

Congo as *La femme profanée*

The British journalist and author Michela Wrong once depicted the Democratic Republic of Congo (DRC) as a paradigm of all that was amiss with postcolonial Africa.[6] The country is big (more than half the size of Western Europe) and is immensely rich in human, cultural, and mineral resources. But President Mobutu's long and dictatorial leadership siphoned off billions of dollars from Congo as its people starved; and from 1996 the country has been embroiled in incessant fighting—the so-called Congo Wars—which have left millions displaced from their homes, over 5.4 million dead, tens of thousands of women raped, and its 67 million people among the world's most impoverished.[7]

An attempt to make sense of Congo's complex history of fighting, which at its height involved the armies of nine countries, multiple groups of UN peacekeepers, and twenty armed groups, confirms the role that founding narratives play in shaping the social history of a nation. For although the actors may be different, Congo's current violence is grounded within the same politics of greed, extraction, and waste of Congolese lives as that of King Leopold's colonial policies, which marked Congo's introduction to modernity.[8]

The more one attends to the ongoing perpetuation of "King

---

[6]Michela Wrong, *In the Footsteps of Mr. Kurtz: Living on the Brink of Disaster in Mobuto's Congo* (New York: Harper Collins, 2001), 10.

[7]See Jason Stearns, *Dancing in the Glory of Monsters: The Collapse of the Congo and the Great War of Africa* (New York: Public Affairs, 2011); Robert B. Edgerton, *The Troubled Heart of Africa: A History of the Congo* (New York: St. Martin's Press, 2002); David Van Reybrouck, *Congo: The Epic History of a People* (New York: Ecco, 2014); and Thomas Turner, *The Congo Wars: Conflict, Myth, and Reality* (New York: Zed Books, 2007).

[8]For a fuller discussion, see Emmanuel Katongole, *The Sacrifice of Africa: A Political Theology for Africa* (Grand Rapids, MI: Eerdmans, 2011).

Leopold's Ghost" in the Congo, the more pressing the missiological question becomes. Can Christianity offer any promise of healing within this social history? What kind of healing? Can it offer an alternative to the social imagination of violence that drives the fighting? What kind of alternative? What makes these and similar missiological questions even more pressing is the fact that more than 80 percent of the Congolese people are Christians.[9] That is why an attempt to explore these questions must start by examining some of the images, prayers, songs, and artistic forms through which Congolese Christians express the nearly inexpressible lament of their suffering and the longing for healing from the violence and its effects.

No image captures this lament and longing as poignantly as *La femme profanée*. Erected by Eugene Sanyambo, a Congolese artist, in March 2008 at Metanoia High School near Goma, the clay sculpture depicts a naked anguished woman, with military boots on her breast, arms, and legs. The black military boots represent the brute force of militarized violence, but they are also empty, thereby pointing to the anonymous and yet ubiquitous violence of the rebels and other armed gangs. That they are torn (with gaping holes where the toes are visible) reflects the vulnerability of the perpetrators of violence themselves (victim-perpetrator; strong-weak dynamics at work with most of the child soldiers).

La femme profanée, by Eugene Sanyambo. Photo by Rebecca Camp, August 2015.

---

[9]Pew Forum on Religion and Public Life, *Islam and Christianity in Sub-Saharan Africa* (2010), http://pewforum.org.

The sculpture operates on a number of metaphorical levels. On one level—the most obvious—*La femme profanée* is a lament for the over 200,000 women who have been raped in Congo.[10] On another level, *La femme profanée* (weak, exposed) represents all the Congolese children, women, and men who have been victims of brutality and violence. And yet again, *La femme profanée* is the Congo itself. In this regard, it is telling that the base on which the sculpture is erected is in the shape of the map of the DRC. It is the DRC, mother Congo, who has been violated, raped, and brutalized through the endless cycles of war.

Another powerful symbol of the sculpture is the lamb in the background. According to the artist, the lamb "represents the symbol of Christ. The woman is leaning on Christ, who remains her last refuge."[11] The presence of the lamb not only provides a Christian interpretative framework, it points to the shared suffering ("com-passion") between *La femme profanée* and *L'agneau crucifié*, between a "crucified people"[12] and a crucified God. In the end, *La femme profanée* depicts the longing for healing of Congo and its people, but also points to compassion as the form that the healing takes. What makes compassion a decisive form of political engagement is the fact that compassion is not merely a private and interior emotion. It is, as Elizabeth Johnson rightly points out, "an empowering power" and a "blazing fierceness . . . that has an efficacy for transformation." Compassion, she writes, is

> an empowering vigor that reaches and awakens freedom and strength in oneself and others. It is an energy that brings forth, stirs up, and fosters life, enabling autonomy and friendship. It is movement of spirit that builds, mends, struggles with and against, celebrates and laments. It transforms people, and bonds them with one another and to the world. Such

---

[10] Jo Adetunji, "Forty-Eight Women Raped Every Hour in Congo, Study Finds." *Guardian*, May 12, 2011, http://www.theguardian.com.

[11] Rebecca Camp, Interview with Eugene Sanyambo, Goma, July 25, 2015.

[12] On the notion of the "crucified peoples" within liberation theology, see especially Jon Sobrino, *The Principle of Mercy: Taking the Crucified People from the Cross* (Maryknoll, NY: Orbis Books, 1994); and Jon Sobrino, *Witnesses to the Kingdom: The Martyrs of El Salvador and the Crucified Peoples* (Maryknoll, NY: Orbis Books, 2003); Leonardo Boff, *Cry of the Earth, Cry of the Poor* (Maryknoll, NY: Orbis Books, 1997); and Choan-Seng Song, *Jesus, the Crucified People* (Minneapolis: Fortress, 1996).

dynamism is not the antithesis of love, but is the shape of love against the forces of nonbeing and death. . . . Neither power-over nor powerlessness, it is akin to power with.[13]

This is the kind of compassion that HEAL Africa represents in the Congo. Co-founded by Jonathan (Jo) Kasereka Lusi and his late wife, Lyn Lusi, HEAL Africa's stated mission is "to compassionately serve vulnerable people and communities through a holistic approach to Healthcare, Education, community Action, and Leadership development in response to changing needs."[14]

Three aspects of HEAL Africa's work stand out and confirm its political engagement as compassion: HEAL Africa as a hospital, a holistic community engagement, and a political imagination. By briefly examining each of these I hope to highlight HEAL Africa's far-reaching impact as a model of mission's critical and constructive engagement in the face of war.

HEAL Africa and the Politics of Compassion in Eastern Congo

A Hospital in Goma

Near the center of the town of Goma in Eastern Congo—not far from the Metanoia High School where the sculpture of *La femme profanée* stands—is an impressive compound that houses the HEAL Africa Hospital. The 200-bed hospital offers specialized and necessary heath care to the local population in and around Goma, where its impact is palpable. In 2014 alone, the HEAL Africa team of doctors treated over 59,000 patients, with over 17,000 consultations; delivered 1,855 babies; facilitated 10 outreach clinics, focusing primarily in the areas of gynecology (over 200 women were treated for fistula) and orthopedics (up to 300 children with club feet were treated).[15]

---

[13]Elizabeth A. Johnson, *She Who Is: The Mystery of God in Feminist Theological Discourse* (New York: Crossroad, 1992), quoted in Kathleen D. Billman and Daniel L. Migliore, *Rachel's Cry: A Prayer of Lament and Rebirth of Hope* (Cleveland: United Church Press, 1999).

[14]HEAL Africa, http://healafrica.org.

[15]HEAL Africa, Annual Report, 2014, http://healafrica.org.

HEAL Africa also serves as a teaching hospital that trains health care providers, and offers general and specialized education, including a family medicine and orthopedic residency training. In 2014, it graduated ten orthopedic specialists, had nineteen others in training, and another fifteen generalists who were enrolled in the residency program.

This focus on medical training and healing reflects much of Dr. Jo Lusi's founding vision. Born in Butembo in Eastern Congo, Jo Lusi studied medicine at the University (formerly Louvanium) of Kinshasa, Congo, and did his orthopedics specialization in Belgium. Returning to Congo, Jo served for nineteen years as orthopedic surgeon at Nyankunde Mission Hospital, before joining MAP International (Medical Assistance Programs—a faith-based nonprofit providing essential medicines for mission clinics and hospitals in developing countries around the world) in 1993 as regional director of health development. He returned in 1994 to Goma, where he co-founded, together with Paul Groen, an American doctor friend, DOCS (Doctors on call for service). At the heart of the DOCS vision was a teaching hospital to train local doctors in the treatment of war-related injuries. Thus, at the height of the 1994 refugee crisis following the Rwanda genocide, and the subsequent start of the Congo Wars, DOCS was literally a field hospital.

More Than a Hospital: A Holistic Program

If the treatment of war-related injuries was at the heart of Jo's initial vision for the hospital, it soon became clear that just treating medical ailments was not enough and that a broader, more radical approach was required. For Jo and Lyn realized that health problems like fistula were often the symptoms of greater social ills. This is when a vision for HEAL Africa was born as Jo and Lyn sought to respond to the drivers of conflict—poverty and poor health in the region—and began working together with local communities. When the Nyirangongo volcano erupted in 2002 and destroyed Goma and the DOCS hospital, the Lusis saw an opportunity not simply to rebuild the hospital, but also to re-envision DOCS as a holistic outreach ministry that came under the name of HEAL Africa. As Lyn Lusi noted:

Lasting change can't be imposed. It can't come from outside. To significantly impact long-term health, disease must be addressed at its roots; the community must be involved and engaged; and cultural values, attitudes and practices examined. So our work is designed to be holistic, providing for people's physical, spiritual and social healing. We do this through Health, Education, Action in the community and Leadership (H.E.A.L) initiatives.[16]

It is this holistic outreach that is reflected in HEAL Africa's mission and extensive programming that covers three broad areas of community health, women's empowerment, and community development. The community health program includes surgical outreach medical clinics (and provides training for doctors and operations for local villagers); *Choisri la vie:* a support program for families affected with HIV/AIDS, using medical support, income generation and savings initiatives; and pediatric care and work with HIV-infected children, mothers, and local communities. The women's empowerment sector includes *Safe Motherhood:* a reproductive health program aiming to reduce maternal and neonatal mortality in seven regional health zones; *Wamama Simameni* (Women stand up together): a network of thirty safe houses offering lodging for women and vocational classes; *Grounds for Hope:* a village for women with irreparable fistulas, enabling them to rebuild their lives in a supportive environment; *Gender and Justice:* an initiative helping villages analyze and discuss traditional practices and customs relating to gender; *Healing Arts:* a program for survivors of sexual violence to learn sewing, therapeutic arts and crafts, soap making, and many other skills, as well as to gain literacy; and *Widows' Solidarity Groups:* cooperative work groups, with income-generating activities, savings, and spiritual support. The community development sector includes such programs as *Guerir mon people* (Heal my people): a program that provides counseling for victims of sexual violence, which complements medical treatment; the *Nehemiah Communities,* which equip village elders and other leaders to help the most vulnerable and to build com-

---

[16]Stuart Harris and Jim Collins, *Love in Action: HEAL Africa* (Freemantle, Aus.: Vivid, 2011), 12.

munity cohesion; nutritional and agricultural training: providing better agricultural techniques through demonstration gardens, helping widows and families grow vegetables and trees for food and profit, and working with street children and ex-soldiers by teaching them life skills, helping them to start businesses, and reintegrating them into the community.[17]

HEAL Africa as Social Imagination

What HEAL Africa's holistic and extensive outreach reflects is a commitment to social repair. The biggest share of HEAL Africa's programming and funding is directed toward the *Wamama* (women's) sector. The reason seems obvious. Women have borne the brunt of the effects of the war. Over 200,000 women have experienced sexual violence. So the healing of the victims of sexual violence represents an urgent challenge. Although the widespread phenomenon of sexual violence in the Congo cannot be reduced to a single factor,[18] it points to an underlying social imagination of plunder, control, and extraction that drives Congo. As Lyn Lusi notes:

Rape has often been used as a weapon of war by various local militias. Sometimes soldiers see it as their right; sometimes they rape to intimidate. If you can make a woman too frightened to go to the field, or to collect water, then you effectively destroy the economy of that village. For warring groups that have wanted to control mining areas—rape is their tactic.[19]

---

[17]Ibid., 42.

[18]The factors behind the widespread rape and violence against women in Congo are complex. Whereas there might be some explanatory power in the usual account of rape as a "weapon of war," such accounts create a limited register for the explication of the violence; the accounts ascribe a rational, utilitarian account to the rape that is often missing from the reality on the ground. "'Rape as a weapon of war' narrative does not match the empirical messiness of war. . . . Congolese military units are scarcely ever disciplined enough to use anything, much less rape, in a systematic fashion" (Maria Eriksson Baaz and Maria Stern, *Sexual Violence as a Weapon of War: Perceptions, Prescriptions, Problems in the Congo and Beyond* [London: Zed Books, 2013], 10).

[19]Harris and Collins, *Love in Action*, 44.

Accordingly, in working with the victims of gender-based violence, HEAL Africa's goal is to get to the underlying social and political causes of sexual violence and not just to treat the consequences. To this end, perhaps more than any program, *Grounds for Hope* provides the most poignant example of the slow, difficult, and ongoing work of social repair under way through HEAL Africa's efforts. *Grounds for Hope* is a village for women with irreparable fistulas, enabling them to rebuild their lives in a supportive environment. Here the women plant vegetables, raise livestock, and engage in other economic activities. Operating in conjunction with *Wamama Simameni* (Women Stand Up), *Grounds for Hope* offers counseling services and education in the areas of literacy, nutrition, HIV, and human rights. Women regain a sense of confidence and the ability to earn an income as they learn practical skills such as soap making, baking, and tailoring. Wounded but now healing, the women of *Grounds for Hope* are an example of HEAL Africa's community restoration effort.

With the establishment of *Nehemiah Communities* in every village where HEAL Africa operates, similar work of social repair is ongoing. Inspired by the biblical Nehemiah who mobilized the returning exiles to rebuild the destroyed Jerusalem, the *Nehemiah Communities* bring together at the village level, religious, cultural, and civic leaders, who like Nehemiah, are committed to rebuilding their communities. The *Nehemiah Communities* thus represent efforts to rebuild Congo from the ground up, one village at a time, undermining the greed, selfishness, and violence that drives Congo's nationalist politics, by sowing a spirit of community concern, the rule of law, the reintegration of rape victims, child soldiers, and other vulnerable members, and offering an ideal of servant leadership. Through the *Nehemiah Communities* Congo is rewired with a new social imaginary.

Ecclesiological and Missiological Reflections

HEAL Africa is an impressive organization whose vision and holistic programs are making an impact in Goma and beyond (over twenty-six provinces are now affected by their work). But what drives HEAL Africa? Or to put the question another way, what is HEAL Africa driving at? Reflecting on these questions offers an opportunity to highlight the evangelistic, ecclesiological, and missiological dimensions of HEAL Africa. For in the end, even as impressive as HEAL Africa's holistic programs are, it is their theological focus that makes HEAL Africa a unique rumination on the church's engagement with the wounded world. Three dimensions of this engagement are worth highlighting.

Practical Evangelism: HEAL Africa as Mission

Even if HEAL Africa's holistic approach grew out of practical considerations, a biblical theological motif underlies it. Asked about the foundation of their commitment to holistic healing, Dr. Jo Lusi points to the text of Luke 4:16–20:

> He has said to set free the oppressed and then to announce the time has come to HEAL Africa; HEAL Africa. You see, that is where we get the vision, how to say our approach must be holistic. When you heal somebody, don't heal only the flesh. You have to heal the heart, you have to heal the soul, you have to heal the person, the family, the couple. You heal the house, you heal the street, you heal the village; you heal the district, the town, the district, the province. You heal the country. You heal Africa the continent. So you see you begin small and then you have to get to the vision of Jesus Christ who pronounced that the Spirit of the Lord is upon me.[20]

In talking about the church as a field hospital, Pope Francis notes: "The most important thing is the first proclamation: Jesus Christ has saved you." Behind HEAL Africa's commitment to perform this Gospel lies a similar evangelistic motif, whose goal is not to convert the people they serve, but to proclaim God's love. As Jo Lusi notes, "We see more than a thousand people every week, who come

---

[20]Jessica Shewan, Interview with Dr. Lusi and HEAL Africa Leaders, Goma, January 19, 2016. All direct quotations from Dr. Lusi, unless otherwise stated, are from the same interview. I am grateful to Jessica Shewan for conducting the interview with Dr. Jo Lusi and other HEAL Africa leaders and for transcribing the interviews.

for treatment. They come for treatment. . . . Our responsibility is not to convert them." The task, he notes, is to "be with those who think they do not have a future, to remind them 'you are sacred.'" Then he adds, "Sacred means you are special; wonderfully made."

In the end that is the good news that HEAL Africa proclaims, or rather *is*, in Eastern Congo.

Ecclesial Radiance: HEAL Africa as a Church

It is not clear that the Lusis, who are Baptists, have ever read or even heard about Francis's theology of the church as a field hospital, but their healing work has brought them to the same appreciation of the church as a field hospital and HEAL Africa as an ecclesial radiance. Thus, continuing to reflect on the text of Luke 4:16–20, Jo Lusi notes: "He wants us to follow his steps, and that is what you call good news. . . . If there is something close to a church according to Jesus, it is HEAL Africa." Asked to elaborate on this insight, he notes, "People call us a hospital. No we are not a hospital. We are HEAL Africa, meaning a church in our understanding, a church that is working, that is doing its job." He talks about the mandate to "heal all types of wounds: not only broken limbs and pierced fistulas, but social wounds, community wounds, economic wounds, spiritual wounds."

In order to heal wounds, Pope Francis has noted how the church as field hospital "needs nearness, proximity. . . . The ministers of the Gospel must be people who can warm the hearts of the people, who walk through the dark night with them, who know how to dialogue and descend themselves into the people's night, in the darkness, but without getting lost."[21] Jo Lusi is aware of the dangers of "getting lost" and complains about the growing danger of neo-Pentecostal prosperity churches in Eastern Congo (which he refers to as "messianic terrorism"). Echoing Francis's positive sentiments, he describes the incarnational vision of HEAL Africa as different: "If you want to help people, you go into the village. You participate; you live with them, you solve the problems with them together."

Given Jo Lusi's description of HEAL Africa as a church it is

---

[21]Spadaro, Interview with Pope Francis.

perhaps not surprising that worship is at the front and center of HEAL Africa's activism. It serves both as the inspiration and glue that holds together their outreach. Every morning patients, staff and visitors at HEAL Africa's headquarters gather together in the chapel to begin the day with worship. Jessica Shewan, my research assistant, describes her experience of the worship service at HEAL Africa thus:

> It was striking to see the joy and energy with which the congregation worshipped. There were "rasta" men who were redeemed from prison by Dr. Jo dancing in one corner with vigor. Then young boys with crutches, who had just received surgery, women who were victims of rape, young street kids, mixed in with doctors and other staff. The worship team included some youth from the choirs, a young doctor in her white coat, and some young men who jumped in halfway, just to dance. Dr. Jo was dancing in his seat. Toward the end of the service, the children's choir was singing "We want to live in your house, all the days of my life."

In the end, it is this "living into God's house" that heals, restores, and renews one's true sense of identity, that HEAL Africa performs in its personal, social, practical, and political dimensions in Eastern Congo.

A Work of Love

At the heart of HEAL Africa is a story of love that has many dimensions. First, HEAL Africa was founded by Jo Lusi and his wife Lyn. HEAL Africa is thus the fruit of the love story between Jo and Lyn: between two unlikely people, a Congolese and a British-born woman, whom Jo fondly remembers as "my queen." They first met in 1971, when Lyn, the daughter of the head of the British Baptist Missionary Society, came to Kinshasa to teach in a mission-founded school. She met a young Congolese medical student, Jonathan ("Jo") Lusi. They were to meet again in Lausanne, Switzerland, where Jo spent a year as a medical intern. They fell in love and were soon married and for the next thirty years, until Lyn's death from cancer in 2012, they stayed together, raised their two children, worked together, co-founded HEAL Africa, and shared a life-long journey of love.

If HEAL Africa grew out of this story of love, what shaped Jo and Lyn's love and drove their compassionate engagement in Congo are two other shared loves. There was the shared love of God, which sent a young British girl, the daughter of the head of the British Baptist Missionary Society, to the Congo in the first place, where she met a young and passionate Baptist Congolese medical student, whose parents were educated by Baptist missionaries. Lyn and Jo also shared a love for Congo, the place that became Lyn's home and where she is buried (Butembo), and fondly remembered as "Mama Lyn." The intersection of these three love stories is in essence the story of mission, which is the story of God's love as it shapes individual lives and vocations, and drives those lives across cultural and geographical boundaries, and thus forms an ever-expanding community of God's family in the world.

The partnership between Jo and Lyn proved to be very powerful for HEAL Africa's success, not least of which was opening up local partnerships to the international development community. But beyond this practical advantage, the lifelong love and partnership between a Congolese man and a British woman radiates a deeper missiological insight, namely that the goal of mission is the coming together of fragments and thus the creation of what the missiologist Andrew Walls calls a true "Ephesian Moment."[22] As Jo Lusi notes, reflecting on their marriage: "Staying with Lyn for a long time, I became white and she became black. . . . So Lyn ended up changing me to become white, and I changing her to become black."

In the end, it is this "new we" that is neither black nor white, neither Congolese nor European, neither male nor female, that reflects the church's true identity and catholicity—and a true Ephesian moment, which is able to reveal "the height of Christ's full stature" (Eph 4:13). It is this "new we" reflected in Jo and Lyn's marriage that is itself a unique historical dynamic and as

---

[22]See Andrew F. Walls, "The Ephesian Moment: At a Crossroads in Christian History," in *The Cross-Cultural Process in Christian History* (Maryknoll, NY: Orbis Books, 2002), 71–87; and see also Emmanuel Katongole, "Mission and the Ephesian Moment of World Christianity: Pilgrimages of Pain and Hope and the Economics of Eating Together," *Mission Studies* 29, no. 2 (2012): 183–200.

such was able to give birth to the reality that we have come to know as HEAL Africa, and which in turn has initiated and crystallized new social possibilities in Eastern Congo—possibilities that reflect God's healing activity in the world.

Maji Matulivu as a Metaphor

So, what does mission's critical and constructive engagement with societies, change, and conflict concretely look like? Like HEAL Africa. And no better image captures this reality than the home of Jo and Lyn Lusi and the guesthouse called Maji Matulivu. The HEAL Africa guesthouse includes apartments and rooms in two buildings overlooking Lake Kivu and surrounded by a stunning flower garden, planted by Lyn. The name Maji Matulivu means "still waters," taken from Psalm 23:2–3. It is appropriate because the sound of water lapping against the wall and the relative calm are a soothing reprieve from the noisy, dusty bustle of Goma town. They are also a reminder that the church's mission and calling in the world is to be a sacrament of God's saving love, or as Pope Francis puts it, it is to "initiative and crystallize processes" that reflect God's compassion in the world. In the midst of ongoing violence and disruption in Congo and other places in the world, HEAL Africa's Maji Matulivu provides a compelling example and image of mission's critical and constructive engagement in a broken world.

Maji Matulivu. Photo by Jessica Shewan, January 20, 2016.

Index